VIRGINS ARE RARE
And Other Important Facts to Remember

Help is here. For centuries, the insider information on how to recall vital facts fast and accurately has been the carefully guarded "secret" (i.e., risqué, outrageous, and ribald) acronyms, rhymes, and epigrams that make up the art of mnemonics. You may be privy to a popular few, such as the old chestnut "Thirty days hath September," but this sinfully revealing compendium collects the best in the fields of music, language, science, history, and mathematics to test your wisdom and sharpen your wit ... while tickling your funny bone all the way to the memory bank.

*Ohm's Law, which states that *Volts* equal *Amps* times *Resistance*.

REMEMBRANCE
OF THINGS
FAST

Test Your Own IQ on the Facts Hidden in These Mnemonic Classics

1. Swiftly Lower Tillie's Pants, To Try Coitus Here.

2. PAIN

3. Lazy French Tarts Sit Naked In Anticipation.

4. Divorced, beheaded, died.
   Divorced, beheaded, survived.

Discover the satisfaction of knowing important (and obscure) facts or just delight in perusing the brilliant, brain-teasing, and downright shocking ways scholars, students, and smart alecks remember the things most ordinary people forget. Susan Ferraro lets you practice your one-upmanship in the game of remembrance and helps you uncover the secret to banishing memory loss forever in this unique and utterly irresistible collection of treasured mnemonic devices.

1. The eight bones of the human wrist are Scaphoid, Lunate, Triquetrum, Pisiform, Trapezium, Trapezoid, Capitate, Hamate.

2. The four nouns in the first declension of Latin that are masculine: *Poeta* (poet), *Agricola* (farmer), *Incola* (inhabitant), *Nauta* (sailor).

3. The nerves that pass through the superior orbital fissures of the skull: Lachrymal, Frontal, Trochlear, Superior maxillary, Nasal, Inferior maxillary, Abducent.

4. Fates of the wives of Henry VIII.

REMEMBRANCE
by OF THINGS
Susan
Ferraro FAST

LAUREL

A LAUREL BOOK

Published by
Dell Publishing
a division of
Bantam Doubleday Dell
Publishing Group, Inc.
666 Fifth Avenue
New York, New York 10103

ISBN: 0-440-20704-5

Printed in the United States of America

Published simultaneously in Canada

November 1990

10 9 8 7 6 5 4 3 2 1

OPM

For the ones who never forget—

Joe

and our children

Mimi and Matthew

CONTENTS

PART 1

...in a single...

...most likely to remember and...

Mnemonic What?

Quick—

Can you name, off the top of your head, the presidents of the United States?

The comedies of Shakespeare?

The planets of the universe, in order, from the closest (and hottest) to the sun to the farthest (and coolest)?

The bass-clef spaces on a sheet of music?

The way to figure out which day of the year Easter falls on?

If you're like most people, in or out of school, the answers are: "It's on the tip of my tongue," "It'll come to me in the night," "Wait, wait, I'm getting it, it's, it's . . . ," and "I'll get back to you."

What you are far more likely to remember, with

a hatred undiminished by time, is the sadistic, fact-crazed teacher who let a cruel smile hover over the corners of his narrow little mouth as he announced: "To pass the course, students must know the kings of England in order *and* the Seven Deadly Sins."

And you will probably remember those times you couldn't remember: the panic, on the exam, when two kings—Henrys?—went AWOL and, having made it a point to remember the deadly sin Sloth, you forgot Anger. (Getting angry at yourself didn't help until six minutes after the exam was over.)

Well, that panic is passé: help is at hand.

Mnemonics—you say it right when you remember to forget the first *m*!—are the silly, usually short, often absurd verbal devices that encode long series of facts that for some reason you have to know. Know them, that is, backward and forward. Cold. As if by rote. In your sleep.

You probably already know some—such as the famous calendar rhyme without which we would all date our checks wrong at the beginning of the month:

> Thirty days hath September,
> April, June, and November.
> February 8 and 20 all alone.
> All the rest have 31,
> Unless that Leap Year doth combine
> And give to February 29.

Most serious scholars scorn such tricks: they sniff that mnemonics aren't real knowledge, they don't teach, and they don't, in and of themselves, mean anything. But those serious scholars are wrong. Mnemonics help people remember what they already know, and if you can't remember what you know, what's the use of knowing it at all?

And mnemonics help people remember what they know *longer*. You might, because you have to, remember the kings of England, in order, for the duration of an exam and for twenty minutes thereafter. But if you know a mnemonic for them—and there are several, so you can choose the one that seems most user-friendly—you'll probably be able to reconstruct the list months, even years later.

Moreover, mnemonics help people remember *all* of what they know *all* the time. The truth is, even if you learn something well, you can forget a part of it temporarily. Mnemonics help people remember complete lists of information; they may be a crutch, but crutches have their uses.

Mnemonics take their name from Mnemosyne, a figure of shadowy allure in Greek myth. Almost nothing is known about her except that she caught the eye of Zeus when he decided he wanted a way to record—that is, remember officially—the triumphs of the gods. (Which means, among other things, that if we didn't already have publicists, the gods would invent them.)

Zeus advocated the theory—or myth, depending on who is doing the talking—that sex solves everything, and it certainly worked for him in this instance. Together he and Mnemosyne produced the Nine Muses, whose specialties (music, different kinds of poetry, history, and astronomy) inspire mnemonics today. Other fields are rife with these shortcuts: medicine, math and—especially—science.

Though some scholars will always disdain mnemonics, they are in one form or another almost as old as Mnemosyne herself. The Greek poet Simonides was an early mnemonist who used a kind of personal instant-snapshot method to remember who was sitting where at a party he'd been to: it came in handy because after he left, the roof fell in and they needed someone to tell which body was which.

Roman mnemonists associated various points in the speech they were going to make the next day with certain familiar pieces of furniture in their home, or buildings on their street. As they delivered the speech, they simply imagined the room or the street, and the ideas they'd attached to, say, the couch or the cornice sprang with smooth conviction from their lips.

In the Middle Ages, when almost everyone was illiterate, easily visualized symbols embodied whole lessons. For the Seven Deadly Sins, for example, Pride was a lion, Envy a serpent, Sloth a bear, Greed a fox, Gluttony a swine, Anger a unicorn, and Lust a scorpion.

But mnemonics as we know them today—jouncing rhymes, smart-aleck acrostics, and frequently addled acronyms—seem to have come into their own with English schoolboys sequestered in their English public (that is, private) schools. They had much better things to do than memorize by rote. They wanted to play games.

So they combined the two—which may explain why there seem to be so many mnemonics for the kings of England. It also explains, at least in part, the characteristically infantile, inane, or idiotic logic that frequently animates them. Mnemonics work best when they are funny, shocking, a little nasty, and occasionally brutish.

According to people who figure out such things, the amount of known facts in the world doubles *every five years.* Memory plays tricks on us all the time, and tends to fade just when we need it most. Turnabout is more than fair play: it's a survival tactic. Remember, a lot of knowledge can be a dangerous thing—if you can't remember it.

Mnemonics to Go

Question: What makes a good mnemonic?
Answer: Sex, slander, and sixth-grade humor.

What every student knows is that if something is bizarre or in bad taste, it's easy to remember; how can you possibly forget what your mother said you're not supposed to mention, not ever? Not only will you remember it, but you will still remember it forty years later.

Do you have to recall in anatomy class the branches of the facial nerve? Just remember the acrostic-style sentence:

Tully Zucker's Bowels Move Constantly

and you will find it much easier to remember Temporal, Zygomatic, Buccal, Mandibular, and Cervical.

Bizarre images also do the trick. Every science student has to remember the geological time periods, usually starting with the oldest and working up to the present. They aren't easy:

Cambrian, Ordovician, Silurian, Devonian, Carboniferous, Permian, Triassic, Jurassic, Cretaceous, Paleocene, Eocene, Oligocene, Miocene, Pliocene, Pleistocene, and (last but not least) Recent.

But consider this peculiar and strange miniparagraph:

Camels Often Sit Down Carefully; Perhaps Their Joints Creak? Persistent Early Oiling Might Prevent Permanent Rheumatism.

It's long and it's odd. In fact, it's ridiculous. But for reasons scientists and psychologists can't quite explain, it's a lot easier to remember than what it stands for.

Mnemonics makers find that the odder the image—the absurdity, for example, of those afflicted camels (although now that I think of it, they do lurch along as if their joints were stiff)—the more memorable it is, while all those big, multisyllabic scientific labels fade and pop from the mind's monitor screen like so many soap bubbles.

So a mnemonic that's funny or absurd works pretty well. A mnemonic that refers to things usually excluded from polite society—the unfortunate Tully Zucker's bowels, bad smells, bodily functions, anyone's underwear, and all things sexual—

works supremely well. For no-doubt-regrettable reasons best unexplored, mnemonics operate most effectively on a sixth-grade level of sexual and social sophistication.

One academic who takes mnemonics seriously is Joel R. Levin, at the University of Wisconsin. He has identified the "critical components of associative mnemonic technique" as the "three Rs": recoding, relating, and retrieving.[1] In other words, a good mnemonic collapses a bunch of disparate material that has to be learned into a new image, connects the two mentally, and then stores the more easily imagined version for quick retrieval.

Making up mnemonics is not hard, though it could be argued that the time spent jiggling a bunch of non sequiturs into a memorable image would be better spent actually learning the—but that way reason lies.

Anything that cues memory counts, even the really ridiculous technique of tying a string on your finger (but how does that remind you of anything other than a string on your finger?). In fact, a more elaborate and successful version of the string on the finger was the army jingle used to help ill-educated farm boys learn to march together before shipping out during World War I. With hay tied to the left foot, and straw to the right, they chanted,

> Hay foot, Straw foot,
> Belly full of bean soup.
> Left, Left, Left, Right, Left.
> First they hired me,

Then they fired me,
Then by golly I left,
Left, Left, Right, Left.

But mnemonics today usually fall into one of four basic types: acrostic-style sentences, acronyms, rhymed jingles (invariably doggerel), and wordplays and puns, which seem especially useful to bad spellers.

Acrostic-style mnemonics are sentences in which the first letter of each word is the first letter of one of the things you have to remember, and the best ones conjure up a visual image: the arthritic camels or Tully Zucker with an unmentionable scowl on his face. Acrostics are good for long lists of things where there is a dearth of words beginning with a vowel.

If the list is shorter, has some vowels, and the word order doesn't matter, acronyms—in which each letter in a word or several words represents the first letter of something to be remembered—do the trick.

For example, what Latin student who has endured the pain of trying to remember which four words, and only four words, of the first declension are masculine, will forget the acronym PAIN? It just happens to include the first letter of the four words in question: *Poeta* (poet), *Agricola* (farmer), *Incola* (inhabitant), and *Nauta* (sailor).

Jingle mnemonics are in some ways the most charming and memorable. Who among us has not learned the most famous spelling rule in English:

I before *E*
Except after *C*,
Or in rhyming with *A*,
As in *neighbor* and *weigh*.

But jingles, even if they are doggerel, are hard to make up if your mind doesn't want to, or doesn't have the rhyming gift. For what it's worth, a lot of rhyming mnemonics come from mathematicians, who seem to be as charmed by the numbered syllables of rhyme as they are by numbers in general.

Finally there are idiosyncratic scraps of wordplay and often low-key puns that can trigger memory. How do you spell *oboe?* If you are spelling-expert Murray Suid, you ask: "Can you play an oboe with your toe?"[2] Suid says that the way to remember how to spell *capital* (and not *capitol)* is to recall that "Cash is a form of capital." But such things are personal: you might find it easier to remember that a capital letter is tall.

Mnemonics makers don't have to be mnemonists, the memory-system experts who develop and promote methods for remembering absolutely everything, including the phone numbers of three hundred people they just met, or their zip codes, or both. But even inordinately gifted mnemonists can and do make use of these home-made devices.

In France there is a seventy-one-year-old businessman named Stephen Van Nest Powelson who has devoted an hour a day for the last eleven years to memorizing the Iliad *in Greek.*[3] Powelson relies mostly on determination and repetition, but he uses, if it helps, some of the shortcuts described here.

Powelson has, among other methods, a kind of personalized acrostic to remember a group of three Greek names that start with *L, P,* and *P:* He remembers them because they are also his sister's initials. It all seems to work; as of September 1989 he'd memorized twenty-two of the twenty-four books, or about fourteen thousand lines.

So always remember to remember this about mnemonics: A lot of would-be mnemonists have gone before you, inventing and adapting hundreds of ways to remember what they have to. Mnemonics become outdated, are often silly and mildly obscene, but the most successful are the ones that have fun.

1. Joel R. Levin, Charles R. Morrison, Julia E. McGovern, "Critical Components," *American Education Journal* 23, no. 3 (Fall 1986): 489–506.
2. Murray Suid, *Demonic Mnemonics: 800 Spelling Tricks* (New York: Dell Publishing, 1990).
3. Judith Stone, "Homer's Greatest Hits," *Discover,* July 1989, pp. 78–84.

ONE

*For Historians Past,
Present, Future, and Until
Five Minutes
After the Exam*

It isn't enough that men and women have to be so active on this small planet—they had to go and invent writing and then, in the fifteenth century, printing. Today we have to cope with roughly four thousand years of recorded history, much of it available to the masses—and this means you and me—for the past five hundred years.

History is facts and dates and names and places. History, in other words, is a gold mine for mnemonics.

They come in rhymes, extremely long and torturous acrostics, and an occasional acronym. They are extraordinarily useful in geography, a field of study that used to be a subject all by itself but is now relegated to a part of social studies (or what-

ever the local educational system chooses to call
it).

British History

1. William the Conqueror, ten sixty-six,
   Played on the Saxons oft-cruel tricks.

2. Divorced, beheaded, died,
   Divorced, beheaded, survived.

The fates, in order, of the six wives of Henry VIII,
who were Katharine of Aragon, Anne Boleyn, Jane
Seymour, Anne of Cleves, Catherine Howard, and
Catherine Parr.

3. The Spanish Armada met its fate
   In fifteen hundred eighty-eight.

4. In sixteen hundred sixty-six
   London burned like rotten sticks.

5. George the Third said with a smile:
   "Seventeen-sixty yards in a mile."

A double mnemonic, this jingle cues both the date
of George III's accession to the throne and the
number of yards in a mile.

The kings of England—all forty-one of them!—
may well be one of the most popular subjects of
mnemonics. Numerous versions are about, and it's
a sure bet that somewhere, possibly in several

dozen somewheres, there are more in the making even as you read. A sample:

6. Willy, Willy, Harry, Ste,
   Harry, Dick, John, Harry Three,
   One, Two, Three Neds, Richard Two,
   Henry Four, Five, Six—then who?
   Edward Four, Five, Dick the Bad.
   Harries twain and Ned the Lad,
   Mary, Bessie, James the Vain,
   Charlie, Charlie, James again.
   William and Mary, Anna Gloria,
   Four Georges, William and Victoria.
   Ned Seventh ruled till 1910,
   When George the Fifth came in, and then
   Ned went when Mrs. Simpson beckoned,
   Leaving George and Liz the Second.

The kings and queens of England, in order, but excluding Lady Jane Grey, are William the Conqueror, William II, Henry I, Stephen, Henry II, Richard I, John, Henry III, Edward I, II, and III, Richard II, Henry IV, V, and VI, Edward IV and V, Richard III, Henry VII and VIII, Edward VI, Mary I, Elizabeth I, James I, Charles I and II, James II, William III and Mary, Anne, George I, II, III, and IV, William IV, Victoria, Edward VII, George V, Edward VIII, George VI, and Elizabeth II. If the present prince of Wales is the next king, he will be Charles III.

For the same general crowd, including Oliver Cromwell and the present prince of Wales, who

will be Charles III, but excluding (again) poor
Lady Jane Grey:

> 6a. Working Wives Have Seldom Had Really
> Jazzy Hemlines. Triple E Rubbers Hardly
> Help. Hairstyles Everywhere Even Resem-
> ble Haystacks, Higher Every Month, Enor-
> mous! Jewish Courtiers Only Clothe
> Jewesses, Whose Men Are Grateful For
> What Virility Endures; Gaudy, Effete Gen-
> tiles Expire, Cheering.

(Note: "Grateful For" represents the four
Georges.)

7. No Plan Like Yours To Study History Wisely
The royal houses of England are Norman, Plantag-
enet, Lancaster, York, Tudor, Stuart, Hanover, and
Windsor.

**8. A Boy Never Will Mistake All The Horrid Bat-
tles Till Bosworth.**
The Battles of the War of the Roses were (St.) Albans, Blore (Heath), Northampton, Wakefield,
Mortimer's (Cross), (St.) Albans again, Towton,
Hedgeley (Moor), Barnet, Tewkesbury, and Bosworth.

9. CABAL
A mnemonic that evolved into a legitimate word,
it stands for the ministers of the English king
Charles II—Clifford, Arlington, Buckingham, Ash-
ley-Cooper, and Lauderdale—who signed a treaty
with France against Holland in 1672. As a word,
this owes much of its success to the similarity with

cabbala, a medieval Latin word used before 1672
to mean intrigue by a small group.

10. Do Men Ever Visit Boston?
The ranks of the British peerage in descending
order are Duke, Marquis, Earl, Viscount, and
Baron.

French History

11. In the 730s, at the Battle of Tours,
    Charles Martel defeated the Moors.

12. Carol Died Clutching Dimwitted Harry's Once
    Valuable Helmet of Brass.

The four ruling families of France were the Carolingian Dynasty, the Capetian Dynasty, the House
of Valois, and the House of Bourbon. For a shorter
version—just Carolingian, Capetian, Valois, and
Bourbon—there's

12a. Cats Catch Vile Bugs.

American History

13. Columbus sailed the ocean blue,
    In fourteen hundred ninety-two.

Americans don't have kings, at least not officially, but they have had forty presidents.

14. Washington And Jefferson Made Many A
    Joke;
    Van Buren Had To Put The Frying Pan
    Back.
    Lincoln Just Gasped, "Heaven Guard
    America!"
    Cleveland Had Coats Made Ready To Wear
    Home,
    Coolidge Hurried Right To Every Kitchen
    Jar
      Nook.
    Ford Cut Right Brow.

The presidents of the United States, in order, are
Washington, Adams (John), Jefferson, Madison,
Monroe, Adams (John Quincy), Jackson, Van
Buren, Harrison (William Henry), Tyler, Polk,
Taylor, Fillmore, Pierce, Buchanan, Lincoln,
Johnson (Andrew), Grant, Hayes, Garfield, Arthur,
Cleveland, Harrison (Benjamin), Cleveland, Mc-
Kinley, Roosevelt (Theodore), Taft, Wilson, Har-
ding, Coolidge, Hoover, Roosevelt (Franklin), Tru-
man, Eisenhower, Kennedy, Johnson (Lyndon
Baines), Nixon, Ford, Carter, Reagan, and Bush.
The first letter of each word in the acrostic para-
graph represents a president, except for Van
Buren, in which both words represent one (Van
Buren himself!). Cleveland appears twice *(Cleve-
land* and *Coats)* because he served two terms, but
not consecutively.

Some mnemonics are best explained by their
inventors. When he heard I was collecting mnemonics, my friend Don Harrison, a former news-

man turned publicist and businessman in San Diego, California, wrote,

"I have been collecting data for a book I would like to write about Jews and the presidency—how each has affected the other—and in a spirit of playfulness I once came up with a sentence for remembering the order of the first sixteen. In the hope that this is not the only thing by me ever published on the subject of Jews and the presidency, I offer the following:

14a. When A Jew Makes Matzo, A Jew Very Happily Tells People That Fortunately Pharaoh Begrudged Leavening.

"Then, for presidents seventeen through twenty-two, one can remember the problems people have transliterating the Hebrew name of a Jewish holiday:

Jews Get Hanukkah Gelt At Chanukah.

"A little bit of Israeli history will aid us to remember presidents twenty-three through thirty-three:

Holy Moses! Remember The Way Hebrews Came Here: Right Through Egypt.

"Finally, presidents thirty-four through forty can be recalled with a sage little saying that indicates that even when things are going right, they can soon go very wrong:

Knowledgeable Jews Never Forget Cain's Remarkable Brother.

"I certainly hope nothing happens to President Bush, because I would surely hate for the world to have to amend the saying to 'Knowledgeable Jews Never Forget Cain's Remarkable Brother Quickly.' "

15. Gentle Virgins who Marry Men claiming New Habits Squelch Caution; Red Indians, Not Yellow, Pursue Nine Chiefs Down Near Jersey.

The thirteen original colonies in North America were Georgia, Virginia, Maryland, Massachusetts, New Hampshire, South Carolina, Rhode Island, New York, Pennsylvania, North Carolina, Delaware, and New Jersey.

A favorite mnemonic of schoolboys in the 1940s and 1950s was

16. ST. WAPNIACL

which stood for the members of the United States presidential cabinet circa 1940: State, Treasury, War, Attorney (General), Postmaster (General), Navy, Interior, Agriculture, Commerce, Labor.

An updated version (the Cabinet has not changed since the Carter Administration) is:

17. ST. DAGIAC Loves Handsome Harry's Silver Handled Umbrella, Dashing Though Extremely Efficient.

The current Cabinet officers are State, Treasury, Defense, Attorney (General), Interior, Agriculture, Commerce, Labor, Health and Human Services, Housing and Urban Development (HUD), Transportation, Energy, and Education.

18. Sliced Black Bread Rarely Stays Moist When Kept Out.

The Supreme Court justices as of 1990 are John Paul Stevens, Harry A. Blackmun, William J. Brennan, William H. Rehnquist (chief justice), Antonin Scalia, Thurgood Marshall, Byron R. White, Anthony M. Kennedy, and Sandra Day O'Connor.

19. Sultry Carol Languished Grumpily Near Carl, Aware Always Virginal Men Frequently Take Time.

The Confederate States of America were South Carolina, Louisiana, Georgia, North Carolina, Alabama, Arkansas, Virginia, Mississippi, Florida, Tennessee, and Texas.

Ancient History

20. Is Perpetual Zeal The Means?

The battles won by Caesar against Pompey were Ilerda, Pharsalus, Zela, Thapsus, and Munda.

21. A True Conservative Can Not GOVern Virtuously; They Do Not Themselves Hate Avarice Altogether.

The Roman emperors were Augustus, Tiberius, Caligula, Claudius, Nero, Galba, Otho, Vitellius (these last three all in the same year), Vespasian,

Titus, Domitian, Nerva, Trajan, Hadrian, Antoninus Pius, Aurelius (Marcus).

22. **Retaliating For Long Frustration, Moses Badgered Hostile Leader Demanding Freedom.**
The plagues inflicted on Egypt as recounted in Exodus, in order, were River of blood, Frogs, Lice, Flies, Murrain (livestock diseases), Boils, Hail, Locusts, Darkness, and Firstborn killed.

23. **Practice Gives Boys Confidence Regarding Male Hormones: Taming Zest, Prolonging Pleasure Alike.**
The Seven Wonders of the Ancient World were the (Egyptian) Pyramids, the (Hanging) Gardens of Babylon, the Colossus of Rhodes, the Mausoleum at Helicarnassus, the Temple (of Artemis at Ephesus), the (Statue of) Zeus by Phidias, and the Pharos (lighthouse) at Alexandria.

Social Studies

24. **Valerie Battles Sin.**
The three main Hindu gods are Vishnu (The Preserver), Brahma (The Creator), and Shiva (The Destroyer). An alternate favored by eleven-year-olds and their teachers is
    24a. **Vampires Suck Blood.**

25. **Sally Just Can't Take Ira's Confusing Black Humor.**
The major religions of the world are Shintoism, Judaism, Christianity, Taoism, Islam, Confucian-

ism, Buddhism, and Hinduism. To include Atheism, add "Anymore."

26. The Kiss That Sheila Allowed Ned Is Still Troubling Alan's Ego.

The months of the Jewish calendar are Tishri (September to October), Heshvan (October to November), Kislev (November to December), Tevet (December to January), Shevat (January to February), Adar (February to March, and a favorite in crossword puzzles!), Nisan (March to April), Iyar (April to May), Sivan (May to June), Tammuz (June to July), Av (July to August), and Elul (August to September).

27. The Four *F*'s

In the U.S. Army the "Four *F*'s" represent what to do when you have hostile intent toward an enemy force: Find them, Fix them, Fight them, and Finish them.

28. Randy Orangutans Take Care During Sex: Heavy Swinging Makes Regular Darlings Propagate.

The animals of the Chinese calendar are the Rat, Ox, Tiger, Cat, Dragon, Snake, Horse, Sheep, Monkey, Rooster, Dog, and Pig.

29. Rotund Flora Squeezed Al's Creampuff Empty.

There are six official languages of the United Nations: Russian, French, Spanish, Arabic, Chinese, and English.

30. POSH

This originally stood for "Port Out, Starboard Home," which requires a little explanation. Going from England to India in the days of the Empire and the Raj, the rich folks sat on the shady side of the boat because, well, they wanted to. Going to India, that meant the right, or port, side, which was the northern side away from the sun. Going home it was the reverse, or the starboard side. From this habit of the rich comes the word *posh*, which today—minus the Empire—still means "elegant," "fashionable," and above all "rich."

Geography: Or, Where in the World Did Malawi Go?

If mnemonics are any kind of indicator, the single most frequently required geographical task, at least in American schools, is to name the Great Lakes.

31. HOMES

The Great Lakes are Huron, Ontario, Michigan, Erie, and Superior. Variants for the Great Lakes, in order, west to east:

31a. **Sergeant Major Hates Eating Onions.**
Or,
31b. **Sam's Horse Must Eat Oats.**

32. AMAH

This word is not only one of the most frequently appearing words in crossword puzzles, but clues the most northern, eastern, western, and southern points in the United States, which are Alaska, Maine, Alaska, and Hawaii. To keep them straight, remember that the word *NEWS* is made of the first letter of the four directions, North, East, West, South.

33. U CAN
The states that make up the "Four Corners" region of the United States are Utah, Colorado, Arizona, and New (Mexico).

34. Not Yearning For Mary's Virginal Devotion, Randy Ivan Plotted Candy's Sexual Conquest; Meanwhile, New Hopes Made Naive Carol Gambol Near Jersey.
The states along the United States Eastern Seaboard are New York, Florida, Maryland, Virginia, Delaware, Rhode Island, Pennsylvania, Connecticut, South Carolina, Massachusetts, New Hampshire, Maine, North Carolina, Georgia, New Jersey.

35. WOW, MA, I CAN MUNCH!
The western states, including Hawaii and Alaska, are Washington, Oregon, Wyoming, Montana, Arizona, Idaho, Colorado, Alaska, New Mexico, Utah, Nevada, California, and Hawaii. A variant in different order, is,

35a. Alone and Naked, Ardent Isabelle Harbored Criminal Wishes While Masticating Nervous Mouthfuls Of Unspeakable Custard.

36. NASA's Astronaut Enjoys Aussie Affairs
    Again.

The seven continents are North America, South
America, Antarctica, Europe, Asia, Australia, and
Africa.

37. Arlene's Best Brassiere Could Cause Every
    Guy Palpitations: Pink Satin Under Velvet.

The countries of South America, in alphabetical
order and including Surinam, formerly known as
Dutch Guiana, are Argentina, Bolivia, Brazil,
Chile, Colombia, Ecuador, Guyana, Paraguay,
Peru, Surinam, Uruguay, and Venezuela.

38. Broken Cesspools Emit Smells, Giving
    Healthworkers New Problems.

The countries of Central America are Belize,
Costa Rica, El Salvador, Guatemala, Honduras,
Nicaragua, and Panama.

39. Crazed Chipmunks Jump Past Nubile Koalas
    Shyly Knitting Mittens.

The countries of the Far East are China (People's
Republic of), China (Republic of), Japan, North
Korea, South Korea, and Mongolia.

40. Bernie Came In Looking Mad, Smashing
    TVs.

The countries of Southeast Asia, as of 1990, are
Brunei, Cambodia, Indonesia, Laos, Malaysia, Sin-
gapore, Thailand, and Vietnam.

41. Beautiful Annabelle's Nasty Mother Banned Blue Silk Panties Indefinitely.

The countries of South Asia, as of 1990, are Bhutan, Afghanistan, Nepal, Maldives, Bangladesh, Burma, Sri Lanka, Pakistan, and India.

42. ST. Paul Marshalled Saintly Con-Verts, Re-uniting Many Christian Ideals.

The islands off the coasts of Africa are São Tomé and Principe, Madagascar, Seychelles, Cape Verde, Réunion, Mauritius, and the Comoro Islands.

43. Excellent Gents Remain Bodaciously Cool, Perplexing Young Hearts.

The countries of Eastern Europe are, with thanks to *Bill and Ted's Excellent Adventure,* East Germany, Russia, Bulgaria, Czechoslovakia, Poland, Romania, Yugoslavia, and Hungary.

44. Barney's Breath Exterminates Great Green Bugs Hanging Motionless Near Gently Swinging Vines.

The large islands of the world, in alphabetical order, are Borneo, Baffin, Ellesmere, Greenland, Great Britain, Honshū, Madagascar, New Guinea, Sumatra, and Victoria.

45. Naked Amazons Mumbling Mayhem Rally Round Young Kings; Outside, Yelling Yeomen Punished Innocent Children.

The ten longest rivers in the world are the Nile (4,180 miles long), the Amazon (3,912 miles), the

Mississippi-Missouri-Red Rock (3,880 miles), the Yangtze Kiang (3,602 miles), the Ob (in Russia, 3,459 miles), the Yellow (2,900 miles), the Yenisei (2,800 miles), the Paraná (2,795 miles), the Irtish (also in Russia, 2,758 miles), and the Congo (2,716 miles).

46. **Adultery Tests Cuckolds Striving To Regain Useful Yang—Generous Vitality Without Tears**

The ten highest waterfalls in the world are Angel (Venezuela, 3,281 feet), Tugela (South Africa, 3,000 feet), Cuquenon (Venezuela, 2,000 feet), Sutherland (New Zealand, 1,904 feet), Takkakaw (British Columbia, 1,650 feet), Ribbon (Yosemite, California, 1,612 feet), Upper Yosemite (California, 1,430 feet), Gavarnie (southwest France, 1,384 feet), Vettisfoss (Norway, 1,200 feet), and Widows' Tears (Yosemite, California, 1,170 feet). For the five highest waterfalls in the world,

    46a. **AT CoST**

47. **Newly Structured Quadrangles By Courteous Mr. PEI Attract New Buyers Needing Office Space.**

The provinces of Canada are Nova Scotia, Quebec, British Columbia, Manitoba, Prince Edward Island, Alberta, New Brunswick, Newfoundland, Ontario, and Saskatchewan.

48. **Why TNT?**

The two territories of Canada are the Yukon Territories *(Why T)* and the Northwest Territories *(NT)*.

49. Catch Queen Victoria Eating Cold Apple Pie. A geographical list required since ancient times is for the Seven Hills of Rome: the Capitoline, the Quirinal, the Viminal, the Esquiline, the Caelian, the Aventine, and the Palatine. Variants include:

49a. Can Queen Victoria Eat Cold Apple Pie?

49b. Poor Queen Victoria Eats Crow At Christmas.

TWO

For Language Lovers Who Think It Might Be Nice to Remember What They Read

Ask literary types what kind of mnemonics crop up in the study of language and literature and they will probably shake their heads in puzzlement or, if they are feeling really witty, quip, "Gee, it's Greek to me." Mnemonics? Theirs is a world of fictional characters who are great precisely because their authors have made them memorable without the aid of mnemonic props.

In fact, an English scholar is more apt to be able to recite Milton's *Lycidas,* as the famous Harvard scholar Douglas Bush was said to have done every morning while he shaved, than to figure out a way to rattle off the novels of Dickens by heart.

Still, most English and language majors have, at some time or another, invented a personal short-cut for a piece of information that didn't otherwise sit comfortably in the brain.

And there are a couple of more pragmatic groups of language students and teachers who seem to enjoy, use, and invent mnemonics. Latin teachers dote on mnemonics, and seem to prefer rhymes, although not always. Teachers of writing find that automatic checklists for coherence help. There are some good ones for French-language students. And English majors? Once aroused, and if desperate enough, they'll try anything.

Classical Literature

Any list of mnemonics for language must begin with a way to remember the Muses, the nine daughters of Mnemosyne and Zeus.

1. Christine Captures Men Every Evening To Tutor Unspoken Pleasures.

Calliope is the Muse of epic poetry, Clio of history, Melpomene of tragedy, Erato of love poetry, Euterpe of lyric poetry, Terpsichore of choral song and dance, Thalia of comedy, Urania of astronomy, and Polyhymnia of sacred poetry.

2. Spectral Willy SAT Proudly Ordering ALE and Peanut Butter.

The seven extant plays of Aeschylus are *(The) Suppliant Women, Seven Against Thebes, (The) Persians, Oresteia—Agamemnon, (The) Libation (Bearers), Eumenides,* and *Prometheus Bound.*

3. Every Prating Baby's Father Tries Keeping
   Calm.

The extant plays of Aristophanes are *Ecclesiazusae, Plutus, The Birds, The Frogs, Thesmophoriazusae, The Knights,* and *The Clouds.*
Those who need a mnemonic for the spelling of
Thesmophorizusae are advised to look deep into
their hearts and make one up.

4. All Airlines Ought To Offer Citizens Is Easy,
   Pleasant Transportation.

The extant plays of Sophocles are *Ajax, Antigone,
Oedipus Tyrannus, Oedipus at Colonus, Ichneutai*
(a satyric fragment), *Electra, Philoctetes,* and
Trachiniai.

English

5. Please Leave Everett's Gory Green Sleeve
   Alone.

Medievalists must memorize the Seven Deadly
Sins, which are Pride, Lust, Envy, Gluttony,
Greed, Sloth, and Anger. During the mostly illiterate Middle Ages, symbols were mnemonics: Lion
(pride), Scorpion (lust), Serpent (envy), Swine
(gluttony), Fox (greed), Bear (sloth), and Unicorn
(anger—not, in this context, virginity).

6. Seven Capable, Young Squires Sailed Merrily
   For France, Knowing Precious Little. Near
   Pretty Calais, Winds Pressed Round, Making

Mischievous Children Puke. Physicians Cre-
ated Several New Medicines.

The pilgrims in Chaucer's *Canterbury Tales* who
told tales were the Shipman, the Canon's Yeoman,
the Squire, the Summoner, the Merchant, the
Franklin, the Friar, the Knight, the Prioress, the
(Man of) Law, the Nun's Priest, the Clerk, the Wife
(of Bath), the Pardoner, the Reeve, the Miller, the
Monk, Chaucer, the Parson, the Physician, the
Cook, the Second Nun, and the Manciple.

To include the all-important Host, Harry Bailly,
add "Huge Boats" after "Winds Pressed Round."

7. Really Capable Knights Sing Glad Ballads,
Capturing Traitors Accused Criminally.

The knight heroes of the six books of Spenser's
Faerie Queene are Red Cross Knight, Sir Guyon,
Britomart, Cambel and Triamond, Artegal, and
Calidore.

8. Hot Tempers Covet Fast Japanese Cars.

The themes of the six books of Spenser's *Faerie
Queene* are Holiness, Temperance, Chastity,
Friendship, Justice, and Courtesy.

9. Senile Cherubs Teach Dull Virtues, Persis-
tently Praising Archaic Attributes.

The nine orders of angels, three in each group,
listed in the New Testament (Eph. 1:21 and Col.
1:16) are Seraphim, Cherubim, Thrones; Domin-
ions, Virtues, Powers; Principalities, Archangels,
and Angels. An alternate:

9a. Stupid Children Tempt Demons, Violating Parental Pacts And Advice.

10. Great Zealots Love New Disasters: Jeering Judges Reciting Sin and Scandal, Kidnappings and Kickbacks, Chaos and Cheats; Encouraged, Men Entertain Joining Proselytizers—Parading Enemies So Slippery Is just Like Ecstasy.

A long but workable acrostic sentence that encodes the first twenty-six books of the Old Testament: Genesis, Exodus, Leviticus, Numbers, Deuteronomy, Joshua, Judges, Ruth, 1 Samuel, 2 Samuel, 1 Kings, 2 Kings, 1 Chronicles, 2 Chronicles, Ezra, Nehemiah, Esther, Job, Psalms, Proverbs, Ecclesiastes, Song of Solomon, Isaiah, Lamentations, and Ezekiel.

11. Donning Halos, Just Angels Ordered Judgments, Making Nine Heavenly Zones House Zen masters.

The remaining thirteen books of the Old Testament are Daniel, Hosea, Joel, Amos, Obadiah, Jonah, Micah, Nahum, Habakkuk, Zephaniah, Haggai, and Zechariah.

12. Matthew Marked Luke's Journey Along Rocky Cliffs while Gallant Exiles Promised Cheer To The Tired, Patient Hebrews; Judicious Planning Justified Joining Relatives.

The Books of the New Testament are Matthew, Mark, Luke, John, Acts, Romans, Corinthians,

Galatians, Ephesians, Philippians, Colossians, Thessalonians, Timothy, Titus, Philemon, Hebrews, James, Peter, John, Jude, and Revelation.

To recall that there are two books each for Corinthians, Thessalonians, Timothy, and Peter, and three books for the second John, remember that

13. **Two Compositions Took The Prize of Three Jujubes.**

(The numbers mean what they say, two and three, and the first letters of the words that follow the numbers match the first letters of the book, Corinthians, Thessalonians, Timothy, Peter, and the second John.)

14. **Michael Groped J. CRUZ**

The Seven Holy Angels are Michael, Gabriel, Jophiel, Chamuel, Raphael, Uriel, and Zadkiel. The angels represented by initials only are mentioned only in the Apocrypha.

15. **Ms. Meany Taught Languid Lassies To Get As Much Midnight Merriment As They Could: Men Elope aT Night.**

A calculating philosophy to be sure, this idea encodes the titles of Shakespeare's comedies: *Measure for Measure, Taming (of the Shrew), Love's Labour's (Lost), Two Gentlemen (of Verona), As (You Like It), Much (Ado About Nothing), Midsummer (Night's Dream), Merry (Wives of Windsor), All's (Well That Ends Well), Troilus and Cressida, Merchant (of Venice), (Comedy of) Errors,* and *Twelfth Night.*

16. Romeo Jogged Through Ancient Hell To Attain A Classic Lesson On Crazed Madmen.

The tragedies of Shakespeare are *Romeo (and Juliet), Julius (Caesar), Titus Andronicus, Hamlet, Timon (of) Athens, Antony (and) Cleopatra, (King) Lear, Othello, Coriolanus,* and *Macbeth.* For *Titus Andronicus* the clue word for *Andronicus* begins with *An,* and for *Timon of Athens,* the clue word for Athens begins with *At.* A shorter acronym for the same titles rearranged is

16a. MAJOR HAL CAT

in which the order begins with *Macbeth* and goes to *Antony (and Cleopatra), Julius (Caesar), Othello, Romeo (and Juliet), Hamlet, (Titus) Andronicus, (King) Lear, Coriolanus,* and Athenian *Timon.*

17. In the alphabet,
    G comes before *S,*
    L before *M.*
    So Gilbert wrote the lyrics,
    Sullivan the music.

This is a way to remember who wrote what in the operatic team of Gilbert and Sullivan.

18. Hairy Dwarfs Decant Great Sherry Bottles Slowly.

For the names of the Seven Dwarfs in the Disney fairy tale *Snow White and the Seven Dwarfs;* Happy, Dopey, Doc, Grumpy, Sleepy, Bashful, and Sneezy.

Rhetoric and Grammar

19. Violet Adopts Aging Cats Needing Personal
    Protection.

The seven parts of speech are Verb, Adjective,
Adverb, Conjunction, Noun, Preposition, and Pro-
noun.

What do you need to remember when writing
an essay or a memo? For Susan Kelz Sperling, a
writing teacher at Manhattanville College in Pur-
chase, New York, it takes

20. GUTS

which stands for Grammar, Unity, Thesis, and
Subordination (of sentences). A variant she sometimes prefers is

20a. GUSTO

or, Grammar, Unity, Subordination, Thesis, and
Organization.

21. COPS

A proofreading strategy developed for learning-
disabled students by Harry L. Dangel, D. Ed., at
Georgia State University in Atlanta, this police image might well help us all clean up our errors of
Capitalization, Overall appearance, Punctuation,
and Spelling.

22. STARS

Another of Mr. Dangel's mnemonics, this one is
for teachers of learning-disabled students (though

rhetoric teachers would do well to remember it too). In working with kids on their writing, teachers need to tend to Structure, Talking (brainstorming alone or in pairs), offering Assistance as well as Reinforcement, and ultimately leading to Self-management of strategies.

23. CATS
A mnemonic invented by Gerard Gindano, this helps students reworking first drafts: Copy a sentence, Alter the words circled by the teacher, Transform the sentences as required, and Supply written answers to the teacher's questions.

Latin

24. PAIN
The only nouns in the first declension of Latin that are masculine: *Poeta* (poet), *Agricola* (farmer), *Incola* (inhabitant), and *Nauta* (sailor).

25. X shall stand for playmates Ten.
    V for Five stalwart men.
    I for One, as I'm alive.
    C for Hundred, D for Five.
    M for a Thousand soldiers true.
    And L for Fifty, I'll tell you.

This handy verse for remembering the value of Roman numerals explains itself (the "D for Five" is 500).

26. In March, July, October, May
     The *nones* are on the seventh day.

Who said mnemonics don't educate? This jingle
encapsulates a whole way of looking at time. On
the ancient Latin calendar there were only three
days that were specifically identified: the *calens*
(the beginning of the month), the *nones* (usually
the ninth day), and the *ides* (usually the fifteenth
day). The Romans counted their days, as they
wrote half of their numbers, by working backward
from known units; thus the fifth day of the month
would be two or four days before the *nones*, depending on whether the *nones* fell on the seventh
or the ninth, hence the need for the mnemonic.
An alternate approach is:

26a. In March, July, October, May,
      The ides are on the fifteenth day.

For prepositions in Latin that take the ablative
case:

27. Put the ablative with *de*,
     Cum and *coram*, *ab* and *e*.
     Sine, *tenus*, *pro*, and *prae*,
     In and *sub* with the ablative case
     Tell about a resting place.

28. She wears a diamond tiara.

In this sentence all the vowels except the last *a* in
tiara represent the vowels used in conjugating the
present subjunctive. For the first conjugation it is
e; the second, *ea;* the third, *a;* the third *-io* verbs, *ia*
(which are conjugated like fourth-conjugation
verbs); and the fourth *ia*. It is with rules like this

that the brilliance, compactness, and necessity of mnemonics becomes crystal clear. An alternate:

  28a. We hear a liar, liar.

  29. After *si, nisi, non,* and *ne,*
    All the *ali*s drop away.

This rhyme tells students that after these four words—*si, nisi, non,* and *ne*—*aliqui* becomes *qui, aliqua* becomes *qua,* and *aliquod* becomes *quod.*

  30. *Dic, duc, fac, fer—*
    Don't look for the *e,* 'cause it's not there.

These are the irregular, singular imperatives of *dicere, ducere, facere,* and *ferre.* A more imagistic alternative is:

  30a. DICk had a DUCk with FER on his back,
    And that's a FACt.

  31. *Sperne -me, -mu, -mi, -mis,*
    Si declinare domus vis.
    (Avoid the endings *-me, -mu, -mi, -mis*
    If you wish to decline *domus.*)

The jingle encodes the rule for getting the forms of *domus* ("house"), which may be declined in either the second or the fourth declension.

A Latin-gender rule that dates from the nineteenth century is,

  32. Males, mountains, months, the winds, the
      streams,
    And people Masculine we deem;
    Isles are Feminine; to these

Add females, cities, countries, trees:
Indeclinables we call
Neuter Gender, one and all.

French

33. An *appartement* in Paris is Perfect.
This is to remember how many *p*'s there are in the
French spelling of the word *apartment*.

34. *English futures have an *e*; French *futurs*
    have none.*
To remember how to spell the word *future* in
French.

35. The indicative is almost infallible,
    The subjective subjunctive only supposes.
When do you use the subjunctive rather than the
indicative? The indicative talks about things that
really happen, the subjunctive is for things one
wishes would happen or that might happen.

36. DR. and MRS. VANDER TRAMP
The irregular French verbs ending in *-re* or *-ir* are:
Dire ("to say"), *Rire* ("to laugh"), *Mourir* ("to die"),
Recevoir ("to receive"), *Sortir* ("to go out"), *Venir*
("to come"), *Avoir* ("to have"), *Naître* ("to be
born"), *Dormir* ("to sleep"), *Être* ("to be"), *Repaî-
tre* ("to feed"), *Tenir* ("to hold"), *Rompre* ("to
break"), *Acquérir* ("to acquire"), *Mettre* ("to put"),
and *Partir* ("to leave").

Library Science

37. Flirting Illusions Please Parents Pursuing Matrimonial Plans For Their Daughters.

One order of listing basic bibliographical detail in book catalogs is Frontispiece, Illustration, Plates, Photographs, Portraits, Maps, Plans, Facsimiles, Tables, and Diagrams.

THREE

For Those Who Need to Spell Gud

Some people are perfect spellers, in which case they can skip this section. Others are so bad they have to check everything, or get a spell-check feature on a word processor, or even hire—as does the big-league Hollywood scriptwriter Stephen J. Cannell—a trusted secretary who can interpret and straighten out the mangled syllables.

But most of us fall into the Great In-Between: We are reasonably good spellers who have four—or four dozen—words that, for no good reason, seem to have misregistered in the brain. Fortunately if you know which words elude you in terms of spelling, you can make up your own private mnemonics.

For fifteen years I misspelled the word *commit-*

ment, putting two *t*'s in the middle, plus the last one. The mnemonic I devised, finally, after embarrassing myself once too often, was the phrase "It takes only two to commit."

In addition to the personal lists, there are famous mnemonics for familiar rules and a few notoriously difficult words. There are two important, easily remembered mnemonics for basic rules, the first of which almost every schoolchild knows:

1. *I* before *e*
   Except after *c,*
   Or in rhyming with *a*
   As in *neighbor* or *weigh.*

For the exceptions to this rule, Murray Suid, one of the nicest, most generous writers currently in business and the author of a book for bad spellers called *Demonic Mnemonics,* came up with a sentence that includes them all:

2. Neither leisured foreign counterfeiter (could) seize either weird height (without) forfeiting protein.

Other familiar mnemonics for difficult words are:

For *Chicago*—

3. Put the *CHI*cken in the *CA*r and the car can't *GO,* that's how you spell *Chicago!*

For *arithmetic*—

4. *A Rat In The House May Eat The Ice Cream.*

For *stationery*—
   5. Stationery uses envelopes.

For *principal* (not *principle*)—
   6. The principal is your pal (but who would believe it?!).

For *geography*—
   7. George's Elderly Old Grandfather Rode A Pig Home Yesterday.
Or, even shorter, more nasty and brutish,
   7a. GEOrge Greedily Ravishes Annabelle Planting Her Yams.

As for a personal list, the words that follow are ones that I've had trouble with at various times over the years. My only comfort is that most of them appear on lists of commonly misspelled words—so I'm not alone!

Even with a mnemonic, the hardest word of all for me is *casserole*, which I wish I'd known how to spell *before* thanking the scores of people who gave me one as a wedding present (I kept putting an *a* after the *ss*). But now I try to think before I write

   8. I eat a casserole.

The rest of my list in alphabetical order:

For *abridgment*, in which the preferred spelling is with no *e* between *d* and *g*, think
   9. It's not a finished *bridge*.

For *acknowledge,* to remember that it does have a *d* (even though a word like *privilege*—see below—does not), think
   10. Deportment *d*ictates acknowle*d*gments.

For *acquittal,* to remember to put the *c* in, think
   11. Acquittal means you *c*an't be tried again.

For *aggravate,* to remember the double *g,* think
   12. Silver *(Ag)* Weight *(gravity).*

For *altar,* think
   13. Angels *a*dorn *a*ltars.

For *alter,* think
   14. Editors alter *e*ditions.

For *analyze,* to remember the *yze,* think
   15. *Analyze* starts and ends like the alphabet, with an *a* and a *y* and a *ze(e).*

For *athlete,* to avoid the misspelling *athelete,* think
   16. *A* *T*all *H*ero *L*oves *E*legant *T*ight *E*lastics.

For *beggar,* to remember the final *-ar,* think
   17. Beggars beg *a*lms.

For *biscuit,* to remember the second *i,* think
   18. *Cui* biscuit *cupit?*
A mishmash of Latin and English, *cui* means *who, cupit* means *wants.* Hey, it works for me: remember, if the mnemonic works for the one who makes it up and uses it, it works.

For *calendar*, to remember the *e*, think
19. *Lend* me a cal*end*ar.

For the extremely pesky *ue* on the end of the alternate spelling of *catalogue*, think
20. Catalo*gue*s keep me *gue*ssing.

For *coarse*, think
21. *Arse* is co*arse* language.

For the absence of a final *e* on the end of *develop*, think
22. *Lop* off the *e*.

For *defense*, which is spelled with *s*, not *c*, think
23. Defen*s*e mean*s* *s*ecurity.

For *embarrass*, because bare asses may be embarrassing but they don't help the word get spelled right, remember all those *r*'s and *s*'s by thinking
24. An emba*rr*a*ss*ment of *ri*che*s* in *r*'s and *s*'s.

For *ecstasy*, to remember the *ecs-* instead of *ex-*, think
25. *e*ating *c*hocolate*s* is *s*ublime!

For *envelop*, which means to surround and enclose and has no *e* on the end, think
26. When *envelop* rhymes with *develop*, lop off the *e*.
For *envelope*, which is a paper container for a letter, think
26a. An *envelope* is *s*ealed on both *e*nds.

For the *br* in *February,* think
  27. *Br*rr, February is cold.

For the *olo* (instead of *ilo)* in *frivolous,* think
  28. P*olo* is for the friv*olo*us rich.

For the preferred spelling of *gray* with an *a,* think
  29. A *ray* of sun will drive away the *gray.*

For the double *m* in *immigration,* think
  30. *I'm m*igrating south for the winter.

For the *gi* in *hygienic,* think
  31. Hyg*i*enic *G.I.* Joe.

For the preferred American spelling of *judgment,*
with no *e* between *g* and *m,* think
  32. Judg*m*ents for and against *General Motors.*

For *knowledge,* which has a *d* in it, think
  33. Knowle*d*ge *d*epends on *d*ata.

For the double *n* in *personnel,* think
  34. John Rockefeller's *son Nel*son.

For *lightning,* which has no *e* between *t* and *n,*
think
  35. *E*lectricity strikes out.

For *preference,* which has no *a* or *i,* think
  36. I have a preference for ease (four *e*'s).

For *pretense* with the preferred *s*, not *c*, think
　37. Pre*tense* makes me *tense*.

For *privilege*, which has no *d*, think
　38. Privi*lege* gives a *leg* up in life.

For *proffers*, think
　39. *P*ublic *r*elations *offers*.

For the double *z* in *quizzes*, think
　40. Too many quizzes make me dizzy.

For the one *c* and the double *m* in *recommend*, think
　41. I write Re: *commend*ations.

For the *s*, not *z*, in *surprise*, think
　42. A*rise* to a surp*rise*.

For the *ymm* in *symmetrical*, think
　43. *Y*oung *m*en *m*ooning look *symm*etrical from behind.

For the inexplicable *ugh* in *thorough*, think
　44. *Ugh!* I hate cleaning thor*ough*ly!

For the *ea* in *treasure*, think
　45. A tr*easure* is *a sure* thing.

For the *lf* in *twelfth*, think
　46. *L*ittle *F*este in *Twelfth Night*.

For the *a* in *villain,* think
   47. The vil*lain* had *lain* dead for hours.
(Compliments to Ms. Gromesky, ninth-grade English!)

For the fact that there is no *e* in *wintry,* think
   48. To *win* you must *try.*

FOUR

For Those Who Do It by the Numbers

Math mnemonics are precise, easy to grasp, and often animated—but not always!—by a pure spirit that is in keeping with a subject that proclaims itself to be pure reason. Many math mnemonics are short verses: either the number of letters in each word corresponds to the number in a series that has to be remembered or the lines just bounce along in evenly numbered syllables.

Judging by the number of mnemonics that explain it, basic trigonometry is what drives most mathematicians around the bend (and forces them to resort to messy verbal memory devices). Of these the most famous is:

Trigonometry

1. SOHCAHTOA

This is an imaginary tribe—or Indian princess or Pacific island—that uses first letters to clue the secrets of trigonometric functions: *s*ine equals the *o*pposite over (divided by) *h*ypotenuse; *c*osine equals the *a*djacent over *h*ypotenuse; *t*angent equals *o*pposite over *a*djacent.

Though some mathematicians prefer to remember the following chart—

$$\text{Sine} = \frac{\text{Opposite}}{\text{Hypotenuse}} \quad \text{Cosine} = \frac{\text{Adjacent}}{\text{Hypotenuse}}$$

$$\text{Tangent} = \frac{\text{Opposite}}{\text{Adjacent}}$$

—along with some other takes:

1a. Oliver Had   A Hairy   Old Armpit.
1b. Oliver Had   A Handful Of Apples.
1c. Oscar Had   A Hunk   Of Apples.

Another variant in which the first letters of the sentence follow the order of SOHCAHTOA is:

1d. Saddle Our Horses and Canter Away Happily Towards Other Adventures.

One that came out of a competition in *Capital M*, the Washington, D.C., Mensa chapter's publication, is:

1e. Sex On Holidays Can Activate Happy Times Over All.

1f. Silly Old Hitler Caught All Hell Through Out Asia.

Other Math Mnemonics

2. By omnibus I traveled to Brooklyn.
The transcendental number *e*, cued by the number of letters in each word, is 2.71828. To the eighth digit remember,

2a. It enables a numbskull to memorize a quantity.

3. The number you are dividing by
   Turn upside down and multiply.
This is the rule for dividing by fractions.

4. Please Excuse My Dear Aunt Sally.
The order for solving algebra equations is Parenthesis, Exponents, Multiplication, Division, Addition, Subtraction.

To find percentages:
5. When *is* comes first
   Take the last into the first;
   When *is* comes last,
   Take the first into the last.
If the question is "Six is what percentage of 100?" then divide 100 into 6. If the question is, "What percentage of 100 is 6?" then divide 100 into 6.

6. **All Students Take Calculus.**
The values of the four quadrants of an axis are All things positive in the first; Sine and cosecant positive in the second; Tangent and cotangent positive in the third; and Cosine and secant positive in the fourth.

Geometry

(And remember, *GEO*rge's *M*other *E*ntered *T*wo *R*aces *Y*esterday!)

7. **O! Eustace is a square!**
To find the area of a pentagon, the formula is
$$A = 1.72a^2$$
where *a* is one side of the pentagon. In the mnemonic, the number of letters in each word represents the number in the formula, the first exclamation point is the decimal, and the five words cue the fact that it is a pentagon.

Barbara Ann Achenbaum teaches math at the Masters School in Dobbs Ferry, New York, and has written a lot of rhymes to help students remember basic geometry facts. For the definition of a postulate:

8. **In geometry, my teacher says,**
   We must prove everything that we state.
   But if it's something we know and just can't
   seem to prove,
   Then we call it a *postulate*.

The protractor postulate rhyme:

9. When Mary found a set of rays, each with an
    endpoint 0
    All lying in the same half-plane, with no
    place else to go,
    She said, "I'll pair the two edge rays with 0
    and 180.
    The rest with numbers 'tween these two will
    have a special matey,
    With ray *OA* match number *X*, ray *OB*, num-
    ber *Y*.
    Then measure angle *AOB*—I'll find it if I try,
    Since *Y* is more than *X*," said she (her
    nerves were all ajangle),
    "*Y-X* has got to be the measure of the
    angle."

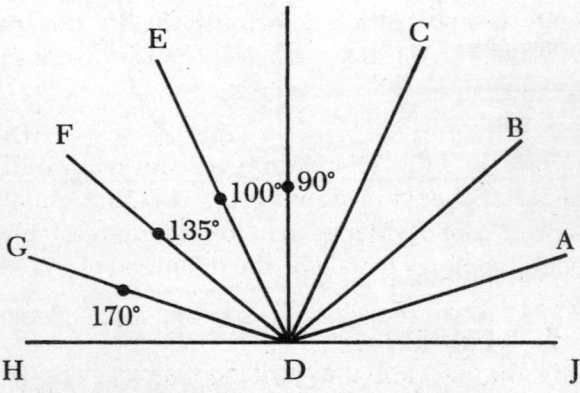

For the definition of a tangent,

10. The tangent leads to a life sublime,
    It meets a circle just one time.

Then on about its business goes,
And where it ventures, no one knows.

For the theorem on right angles,

11. A tangent met a circle at just one point
called *L*,
A radius of that circle went through that
point as well.
The greatest thing about these lines is not
just that they meet,
But that they form right angles,
A most ingenious feat.

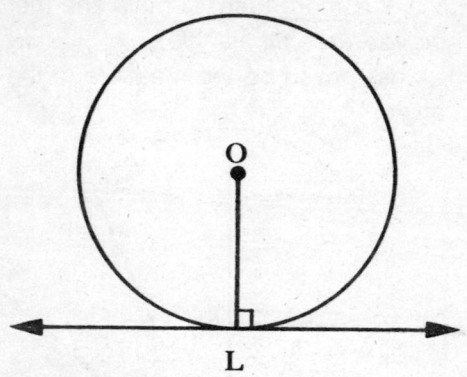

The definition of a chord is

12. "You're really not so special," circle *C* told
chord *AB*.
"You're merely just a segment with your
endpoints both on me."

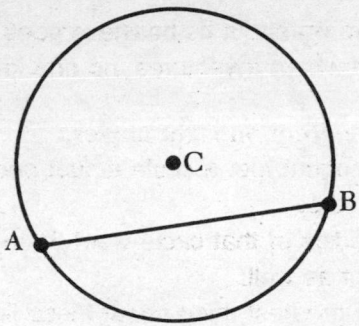

A theorem on chords is

13. Here's a fact about a circle that's an easy
    one to tell.
    If these two chords are congruent, their
    arcs must be as well.

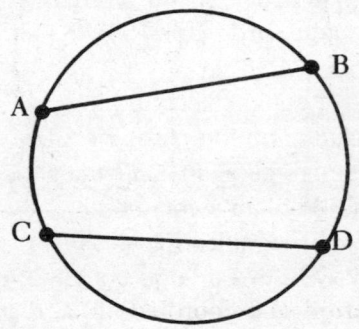

A theorem on inscribed angles is

14. To measure an inscribed angle doesn't
    require much wit,
    Just find its intercepted arc, and then take
    half of it.

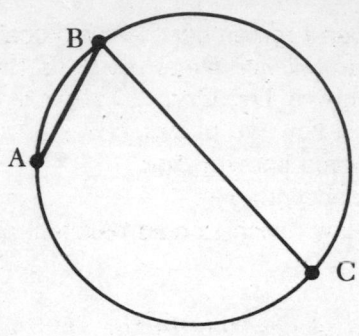

$$m < ABC = 1/2 \ m \ AC$$

The value of pi seems to hold eternal fascination for those who live for numbers. A host of mnemonics give the number to ever-greater decimal places. This mnemonic verse gives pi to the twentieth decimal place, taken from the number of letters in each word—3.14159265358979323846.

15. Pie,
   I wish I could calculate pi,
   Eureka! cried the great inventor,
   Christmas pudding, Christmas pie
   Is the problem's very center.

For pi to eight significant places:

15a. May I have a large container of coffee?

To fourteen places (rounded off, and spelling *Archimedes* with an *x*):

15b. How I wish I could recollect of circle round
   The exact relation Arximedes propound!

For the reciprocal of pi (rounded off, 3.18310), try counting the letters in

15c. Can I remember the reciprocal?

Writing in *Science Digest* in 1983, the mysterious and elusive Dr. Crypton reported other pi mnemonics. For five places, try

15d. Yes, I know a digit.

For nine places, there's

15e. How I wish I could recollect pi easily today.

For eleven places, there's the 1926 *Chambers's Encyclopedia* entry, which uses the English spelling of *endeavor:*

15f. But I must awhile endeavour to reckon right the ratios.

For thirteen places:

15g. Now I live a drear existence in ragged suits and cruel taxation suffering.

An alternate for thirteen places in rhyme (with a double *t* in *ofttimes*),

15h. See, I have a rhyme assisting
My feeble brain, its tasks ofttimes
resisting.

A similar, but longer, rhyme gives pi to twenty-one places (the twenty-first place is six):

15i. Sir, I send a rhyme excelling
In sacred truth and rigid spelling
Numerical sprites elucidate
For me the lexicon's dull weight.

Dr. Crypton also unearthed rhymes for pi to thirty-one places (3.14159265358979323846264 3-

383279) in three languages. The best of the English, the result of a 1951 mnemonic contest held in the company publication of Lloyds Bank International under the direction of Lord Balfour of Burleigh, is

15j. Now I will a rhyme construct,
By chosen words the young instruct,
Cunningly devised endeavor.
Con it and remember ever
Widths in circle here you see
Sketched out in strange obscurity.

FIVE

*For the Musically
Inclined (or the
Musically Supine,
Depending on the Hour)*

Playing music is one thing, knowing how to read music quite another. Musicians—usually beginning musicians—often rely on acrostics and acronyms that help them learn how. The multitude of mnemonics for the notes of the treble-clef lines suggests that whether a student is six or sixty, this may be the single hardest thing music makers have to know.

1. **Elephants Got Big Dirty Feet.**
The notes of the treble-clef lines are E, G, B, D, F. Variations include:

1a. **Every Good Boy Does Fine**
which music teachers over the age of thirty proba-

bly hum in their sleep. For chocolate lovers, there's

1b. Every Good Boy Deserves Fudge.

Those who love the ludicrous would do well to remember

1c. Elephants Go Belly Dancing Fridays.

And a phrase that is uttered with heartfelt sighs by preadolescents is

1d. Empty Garbage Before Dad Flips.

2. STAB

The four major voice parts are Soprano, Tenor, Alto, and Bass.

The notes of the treble-clef spaces are

3. FACE

For the bass-clef spaces, A, C, E, and G:

4. All Cars Eat Gas.

A more rural variation:

4a. All Cows Eat Grass.

5. Girls Buy Dolls For Amusement

The notes of the bass-clef lines are G, B, D, F, and A.

6. Frederick Charles Goes Down And Ends Battle.

The order in which sharps are entered in key signatures is F, C, G, D, A, E, B. Reverse the order for flats. A variation is:

6a. Five Cats Got Drowned At East Boston.

7. BEAD

This is a double-barreled mnemonic that clues the short list of the flats *and* the cycle of fifths, a common harmonic movement (B moves to E, E moves to A, A moves to D).

8. Early Birds Grab Dozing Animals' Eggs.

The open strings on the guitar are E, B, G, D, A, and E.

Paul Morris of Tempe, Arizona, knows a lot about music. Some of his favorite mnemonics include familiar opening melodies that clue certain musical intervals.

9. "Here comes the bride . . ."

This familiar combination of notes clues the interval of a fourth (C to F).

10. "Ma-ri-a . . ." (from *West Side Story*)

Hum this for the interval of a tritone, C to F-sharp.

11. "My bonnie . . ." (from "My Bonnie Lies Over the Ocean")

This is for the interval of a sixth (C to A).

12. The seventh must go down,
    The seventh must go down.
    Hi, ho, the derry-o.
    The seventh must go down!

Sung to the nursery tune "Hi, ho, the derry-o," this jingle teaches beginning students to resolve the seventh in basic four-part harmony.

13. Don't double the leading tone!

This cautions students never to have two voices on
the leading tone (the seventh note of a diatonic
scale).

SIX

Mnemonics That Fly for Legal Eagles

Legal eagles construct mnemonics that are direct, practical, and index all manner of human skullduggery (and what a lawyer can do about it), particularly as it applies in their geographical jurisdiction. What is required to get a divorce? Who owns what under which circumstances? Who gets the money when someone dies?

Most of the time lawyers can look up what they need to know in books. But there are two times in their lives—on the bar exam and when standing before a judge in a courtroom—when they need to know answers cold, immediately, and without hesitation. Instant legal acumen tripping off the tongue also impresses clients and saves time. Who wants to spend all day looking things up in the library?

Legal mnemonics are unlike other mnemonics in two ways: All of them are acronyms, and the acronyms in almost all cases require lengthy explanations. Face it: One of the measures of a good attorney is his or her ability to dazzle not only with strategy, but with the sheer multitude of syllables that seem to pour forth on a half-second's notice. These mnemonics—all but three of which (1, 15, and 16) are from a bar-review course (see below)— are no exception.

1. MR. and MRS. LAMB
The nine felonies in common law are Murder, Rape, Manslaughter, Robbery, Sodomy, Larceny, Arson, Mayhem, and Burglary.

J. Gardiner Pieper, a lawyer in New York, has been giving the Pieper Law Review Course for that state's bar exam since the early 1970s. In his spare time he takes bar exams himself, all over the country; he is now admitted in sixteen states.

For himself and his students Pieper has found that mnemonics work. "I'll run into former students sometimes at the courthouse ten years later, and they say they still remember them," he said. In all there are some 170 or so Pieper mnemonics.

2. BACH'S PIES
In the Fourth Amendment the framers of the United States Constitution prohibit unreasonable searches (i.e., without a warrant). There are certain exceptions, however, and these are the following: Border searches; in Automobiles (if probable cause); in Consent searches (if the person being

searched agrees); in Hot-pursuit searches (if the police are apprehending a dangerous criminal on the run); in School searches (authorities have the right to open school lockers and search pockets without a warrant); in Plain-view searches (when police can see something in plain view on, for example, the seat of a car); in a search Incident to a lawful arrest; in Emergency searches in exigent circumstances (for example, if there is a fire in the house and the police come in without a warrant); and in constitutional Seizures—stop and inquire, stop and frisk, and stop and arrest (which last requires probable cause that a person has committed a crime).

3. SWEPT

In New York the rules governing a will are very strict. The will must be Signed by an adult (someone over the age of seventeen); it must be in Writing (not an oral declaration); the signature must be at the End (postscripts don't count); it must be Published (the testator must state orally that this is his will); and finally it must be witnessed by Two disinterested parties (people not left anything in the will).

4. MAD "CAR" CLAW

This is the car that drives in when there is a valid will and there have been events since the signing that affect it: Marriage of the testator; "Afterborn" children (children born later); Divorce; Common disaster for both testator and beneficiary (both killed in an airplane crash, for example); Ad-

vancement (when the testator gives some of the
inheritance to beneficiary before death); Renunci-
ation by beneficiary (usually for tax purposes); Cy
pres (for charitable bequests to charities that have
shut down since the will was made); Lapsed lega-
cies (when the beneficiary predeceases the testator); Ademption and abatement (when the item
left in the will has been lost or destroyed and can't
be given to the inheritor); and Wrongful act of
beneficiary (if the heir kills the testator, he cannot
inherit).

5. A MILD Court

The proper methods for serving a summons are
the following: serving the defendant's Agent; serving by Mail if the defendant consents (it must be
acknowledged); In-hand delivery; Leaving it with
a SAD (Suitable Age and Discretion) person and
mailing it also; after Due diligence, going the
"nail, mail, and file" method (after several at-
tempts at different times), affixing it to the door
with tape (not a real nail), mailing it, and filing
proof of service with the court; and if all else fails,
asking the Court to prescribe a method (usually it
is to serve by publication in a newspaper).

6. CRIB PIC

A witness can be impeached on cross-examination
by Contradiction; by having a bad Reputation; by
being known to have committed Immoral, vicious,
or criminal acts (if a witness can be shown to have
filed a fraudulent tax return, for example, that is
proof that he puts himself before the law); by Bias

of the witness; by a Prior inconsistent statement; by Influence of drugs or alcohol; and by prior Criminal conviction of a witness (very devastating).

7. PAID SEAT

The things you have to take into account for determining equal distribution on a divorce, excluding marital property, are the following: Property (separate); Age and health; Income earned by each; Duration of marriage; Standard of living of parties; Earning capacity; Any other relevant factor; and Tax consequences.

8. A PAIN

Grounds for divorce in New York are Adultery, Prison (imprisonment for three years), Abandonment, Inhuman (and cruel) treatment, and No-fault conversion divorce.

9. CRAP

When defending against an adultery charge, a party in a divorce can argue any of the following: Condonation (which means that the other party forgave the adultery at the time, or at least slept with the adulterer again after knowing about it); Recrimination (they were both fooling around); Act of adultery (a vague item on the list, but loosely referring to the fact that adultery doesn't count in law, at least if it happened more than five years previously); and Procurement or connivance of the other spouse (in the old days, when adultery was the only grounds for divorce in New York, couples would sometimes cooperate in arranging grounds).

10. A MAC DOG
To get jurisdiction over a company, a lawyer must serve one of the following: an Assistant cashier, a Managing agent, an Agent express or implied, a Cashier, a Director, an Officer, or a General manager.

11. LIAR
The four provisional remedies—things a lawyer can do while a case is in progress to preserve the property or ensure the enforceability of a judgment when (and if) it happens—are Lis pendens, Injunction, Attachment, and Receivership.

12. MOP
Requirements for due process when seeking jurisdiction over a defendant are Minimum contacts (of defendent within jurisdiction), Opportunity (of the defendant) to be heard, and Proper process in terms of service of notices, and so forth.

13. DIAL D.C.
To get jurisdiction over a person in the state of New York, attorneys must show that the person has been Doing business (in the state); has In hand service of process in the state; that an Agency situation exists (that is, if the person appoints an agent for service of process in New York); that Long-arm jurisdiction rules apply; that the Domicile is in the state; or that Consent is given to the jurisdiction.

14. SIR EAT DAMP

Some exceptions to the hearsay rule are the following: <u>S</u>tate of mind of the speaker; <u>I</u>mpression (present sense impression); the business <u>R</u>ecord; <u>E</u>xcited utterance; <u>A</u>dmission by a party; former <u>T</u>estimony; <u>D</u>ying declaration; declaration <u>A</u>gainst interest; <u>M</u>iscellaneous; and <u>P</u>edigree (statement of relationships).

English Law Division

15. SAFES

The powers of the mortgagee under the 1925 Property Act in England are <u>S</u>ue, <u>A</u>ppoint receiver, <u>F</u>oreclose, <u>E</u>nter into possession, and <u>S</u>ell.

16. ERICS

The five kinds of Trusts in English Law are <u>E</u>xecutory, <u>R</u>esulting, <u>I</u>mplied, <u>C</u>onstructive, and <u>S</u>tatutory.

SEVEN

The Body Specifics—
Medicine and Anatomy

Hospitals are not realms of polite society—which no doubt explains why doctors and medical students, surrounded as they are by flesh and mortality, so often think of sex. When they aren't being lascivious, they tend toward the gross.

It's understandable. People who will be doctors —who sign on for a life of probing innards, sticking needles into warm, smooth flesh, thumping the innocent kidney, cutting through skin and sawing bones—are not like most people to begin with.

To be fair, what they have to remember is daunting: oodles of polysyllabic stuff that most of us can't even pronounce. It's not just the bones in the body but the nerves and muscles and systems and germs, the illnesses, the options, and the probable outcomes.

All that does not quite explain, however, why

medical mnemonics are full of so much—well—
appallingly bad taste. They are also frequently sexist. It might be said that in prefeminist days, when
many of these mnemonics came into being, medicine was dominated by men who didn't know better.

Yet my best informant for this category of mnemonics was my own doctor, a woman. Her hus-
band, also a doctor, was too embarrassed to tell me
half of the ones he knew. So go figure.

Whatever the reason, here are mnemonics that
almost every doctor knows and every patient, having once heard, remembers.

Anatomy

1. Lazy French Tarts Sit Naked In Anticipation.
The names of the nerves that pass through the
superior orbital fissure of the skull: Lachrymal,
Frontal, Trochlear, Superior, Nasal, Inferior, and
Abducent.

2. SKILL
The excretory organs of the body are Skin, Kid-
neys, Intestine, Liver, and Lungs.

3. On Old Olympia's Towering Tops,
   A Finn And German Vault And Hop.
The twelve pairs of cranial nerves are Olfactory,
Optic, Oculomotor, Trochlear, Trigeminal, Abdu-
cent, Facial, Auditory, Glossopharyngeal, Vagus,
Accessory, and Hypoglossal. Variations abound.
There's the World War II version:

3a. On Old Olympia's Towering Tops
   A Fat-Assed German Vaults And Hops.

The nurse's polite version:

3b. On Old Olympus's Towering Tops
   A Finn And German Vault A Hedge.

But the least forgettable of all, of course, is the very lonely-medical-student-guy version:

3c. O, O, O, To Touch And Feel
   A Girl's Vagina—
   Ah, Heaven!

4. Oh, Be Darned!

A tame high school anatomy class mnemonic for the path of the facial nerve in the facial canal—Outward, Backward, and Downward.

5. Missing Bird Left, Mammal Right.

When probing a "mystery" chest—if you can imagine just happening to come across a stray cadaver of unrecognizable origin and deciding to look into it—it helps to know that the difference between a mammal and a bird is that if the main blood vessel leaving the heart turns to the left, it's a bird; if it turns to the right, it's a mammal. Who said mnemonics weren't useful?

Another description of anatomical arrangement is,

6. The Lingual Nerve
   Takes a swerve
   Around the hypoglossus,

While "I'll be f——d,"
Says Stenson's duct,
"The son of a bitch
Swung around us!"

7. Some Criminals Have Underestimated Royal
   Canadian Mounted Police.
The bones of the upper limb are the Scapula,
Clavicle, Humerus, Ulna, Radius, Carpals, Meta-
carpals, and Phalanges.

8. Help For Police To Find The Missing Persons.
The bones of the lower limb are Hip, Femur, Pa-
tella, Tibia, Fibula, Tarsals, Metatarsals, and Phalanges.

9. Never Lower Tillie's Pants, Mother Might
   Come Home.
The eight bones of the human wrist (circa 1940)
are: Navicular, Lunate, Triquetrum, Pisiform,
Multangular greater, Multangular lesser, Capitate,
and Hamate.

Some of the names of the bones had changed by
the 1960s, necessitating the following:
    9a. Swiftly Lower Tillie's Pants, To Try Coitus
        Here.
Scaphoid, Lunate, Triquetrum, Pisiform, Trapezium, Trapezoid, Capitate, Hamate.

10. Tully Zucker's Bowels Move Constantly.
An unfortunately unforgettable way to remember
the branches of the facial nerve—Temporal, Zygomatic, Buccal, Mandibular, and Cervical.

11. RED MEN CRIS

The ten systems of the human body are Reproductive, Execretory, Digestive, Muscular, Endocrine, Nervous, Circulatory, Respiratory, Integumentary, and Skeletal. A variant, with a different order:

11a. NERD CRIMES

Medical Practice

12. Bones, stones,
     Abdominal groans
     And mental moans.

The symptoms of hypercalcemia (an excess of calcium in the blood) include aching bones, stomach pains, and mental upset.

13. NAVEL

A word (and image) used by doctors wishing to distinguish (as well they might!) a vein from the artery when drawing blood. These slippery, wiggly shapes can be felt under the skin, moving from the pelvis to the lower abdomen—Nerve, Artery, Vein, Empty space, Lymphatic.

14. Clever Dick Loves Silly Chloe.

An essential mnemonic for anyone with back problems, or diagnosing same, this cues the vertebral bones of the spinal column—Cervical, Dorsal, Lumbar, Sacrum, and Coccyx.

15. RICE
Recommended treatment for sprained ankles: Rest, Ice, Compression, and Elevation.

16. BULL
A dentist's clue for "Buckle of the Upper, Lingual of the Lower," which describes the cusps adjusted when fitting dentures.

17. SASH
The order of infusing antibiotics intravenously is Saline, Antibiotic, Saline, and Heparin.

18. O VESALIUS!
Vesalius was the Flemish anatomist who was among the first to describe the spine in detail, and the letters of his name list most of the serious things that can go wrong with a spine: Osteomyelitis, Vertebral fracture, Extra-spinal tumors, Spondylolisthesis, Ankylosing spondylitis, Lumbar disk disease, Intraspinal tumors, Unhappiness, and Strain.

19. D.C. VAN DISSEL
In admitting a patient to the hospital, the doctor sees to and defines or orders Diagnosis, Condition, Vital signs, Ambulation, Nursing orders, Diet, Intake and output, Symptomatic drugs, Specific drugs, Examinations, and Laboratory work.

Robert Bloomfield, M.D., is an assistant professor at the Bowman Gray School of Medicine, Wake Forest University, Winston-Salem, North Carolina, and also a collector and publisher—in *Mnemonics, Rhetoric and Poetics for Medics* and its sequel—of medical mnemonics. The following are from among the hundreds this generous and friendly man has amassed (I've simplified the lengthy medical explanations he gives):

20. LIMP PENIS
The causes of impotence are Lassitude, Injury to penis or genital area, Medications, Peyronie's disease, Priapism, Endocrine disorders, Neurologic disorders, Ischemia, and Supratentorial causes (depression, anxiety, marital discord, and the like).

21. AEIOU
The vowels stand for the possible causes of acute pelvic pain in women; Appendicitis, Ectopic pregnancy, Infection (pelvic inflammatory disease), Ovarian cyst, and Ureteral (kidney stone lodged in ureter).

22. DEFIANCE
The clinical features of Lyme disease are suspected geographical Distribution (the Northeast); *Erythema chronicum migrans* (the rash); Fever; *Ixodes damminni* (the tick); Arthritis; Neurologic manifestations (can include meningitis or encephalitis); Cardiac abnormalities; and Episodic nature of flare-ups.

23. CLAP CATCHES UP
The sites of involvement with gonorrhea are Cervicitis, Lymphadenitis, Arthritis, Pharyngitis,

Conjunctivitis, Abscesses, Tubal infections, Central nervous system involvement, Hepatitis, Endocarditis, Skin lesions, Urethritis, and Proctitis. Ugh.

24. CAIN HAD HUGE FITS
Remind yourself that Cain attacked Abel and that fits (or seizures) are often called attacks, and you will remember that the causes of seizures are Cerebrovascular disease, Axnoia, Idiopathic epilepsy, Neoplastic disorders (brain tumors), Hysteria, Alcoholism, Drug use, Hepatic insufficiency, Uremia, Glucose hypoglycemia, Electrolyte disturbances, Febrile seizures, Infections, Trauma, and Shunts.

25. OLD HEART
Preexisting conditions that a physician should look for when prescribing digitalis, since they might cause adverse reactions, are Old age, Liver disease, certain Drugs, Heart disease, Electrolyte disturbances, Acidosis, Renal insufficiency or failure, and Thyroid disease.

26. I CHOP
Indications for surgery in cases of inflammatory bowel disease are Infection, Carcinoma, Hemorrhage, Obstruction, and Perforation.

27. AS I PREP A BOWEL
The causes of malabsorption are Absorptive surface bypass, Sprue (a chronic disease marked by

fatty diarrhea and deficiency syndromes), Inflammatory bowel disease (Crohn's disease), Pancreatic insufficiency, Radiation enteritis, Enzyme deficiency, Parasites, Amyloid, Bile salt deficiency, Overgrowth of bowel bacteria, Whipple's disease, Endocrine causes, and Lymphoma.

28. PIMPLED ASS

The causes of diffuse hyperpigmentation are Primary biliary cirrhosis, Iron overload, Malignant melanoma, Porphyria, Liver disease, Endocrine causes, certain Drugs, Arsenic, Scleroderma, and Sprue.

29. ABSENT APLOMB

The causes of vertigo and disequilibrium are Arrythmias, Blood pressure elevation or depression, Subclavian steal (involving the reversal of blood flow in the vertebral artery), Epilepsy, Neuronitis, Trauma, Acoustic neuromas, Paroxysmal positional vertigo, Labyrinthitis, Ototoxins, Menière's disease, Basilar migraine or ischemia. As if this weren't bad enough, the list *excludes* several other causes of vertigo—lateral medullary syndrome, cerebellar hemorrhage or infarction, and multiple sclerosis.

30. CHANCReS = GUILT

Sexually transmitted diseases are Chlamydia, Herpes, Amebiasis, *Neisseria gonorrhoeae*, *Condyloma acuminata* (venereal warts), Reiter's syndrome (not a cause but a contributing factor), Syphilis, Granuloma inguinale, *Ureaplasma urealyticum,* Infectious hepatitis, Lice (and scabies), and trichomoniasis. And yes, there are omissions from this list too: chancroid, AIDS, and *Haemophilus vaginalis.*

    31. Hot as a hare,
         Mad as a hen,
         Blind as a bat,
         Red as a beet,
         Dry as a bone.
The symptoms of belladonna poisoning are temperature elevation, restlessness and occasional delirium, blurred vision, flushed skin, and dry mouth and skin.

Enough!

EIGHT

*For Stargazers and
Other Pursuers of
Scientific Truths—
Biologists,
Paleontologists,
Geologists, Physicists,
and Chemists*

How do you feel when you have to remember too many polysyllables, belonging to too many complicated categories? How do you feel when what you do all day is serious, important stuff?

You may feel like a scientist who is very grateful for any mnemonic he (or she) can wrap his (or her) brain around—especially if it is funny, or just silly enough to provide a certain irrational relief.

To judge by the mnemonics that abound in the different areas of science—and there are more for the sciences than for any other field—scientists dote on wackiness and delectable illogic. It's understandable: They do not, like English majors, get to take a break from the heavy stuff and do a paper on, say, the comedic elements of the periodic table. So they appreciate what can only be called a refreshing change of pace.

True, the humor is often a little adolescent. But adolescent humor is what makes mnemonics work, so all those dorky jokes have a useful purpose.

Besides, what do you expect from a group that has spent every waking moment since the age of eight assembling strange, complicated devices and then taking them apart? As my friend Carmen Cole observed, after reading over a bunch of mnemonics remembered by her scientifically oriented family, "You will probably decide, on the basis of the list, that neither of our daughters should go out with electrical engineers (a sexist group if their chief mnemonic is any indication); astronomers are a gentler lot, so it's probably okay."

Here's that most offensive mnemonic, which electrical engineers almost always learn:

1. Bad Boys Rape Our Young Girls, But Violet Gives Willingly.

The color of the bands on electrical resistors, with a value of 0 through 9 in the order given, are Black, Brown, Red, Orange, Yellow, Green, Blue, Violet, Gray, and White.

Nonsexist, nonabusive alternates for those who did happen to notice that women's liberation took place some time ago:

1a. Better Be Right, Or Your Great Big Venture Goes West.

Or, for those who are into women's rights but not animal rights (and who appreciate a haikulike quality, albeit in twenty syllables):

1b. Black Birds Racing
    Over Yellow Grass
    Behind Violet Garden
    Walls Get Shot.

Another electrically wired mnemonic is:

2. Virgins Are Rare.

Ohm's law states that Volts equal Amps times Resistance.

There are so many other mnemonics for the sciences that they have to be divided up into categories.

Basic Chemistry

3. Mere Kisses Seem Ample—Keep Me Cuddled!

An essential first step in tackling chemistry problems is to know the units of the International System of Measurements, or Meter, Kilogram, Second, Ampere, Kelvin, Mole, and Candela. A useful companion mnemonic follows.

4. Kids Have Dropped Over Dead Converting Metrics.

The prefixes used in metric units are Kilo-, Hectar-, Deka-, Origin-, Deci-, Centi-, and Milli-.

5. Mary Eats Peanut Butter.

The first four hydrocarbons of the alkane class are Methane, Ethane, Propane, and Butane, in ascending order of the number of carbon atoms in their chains. These four are frequently used in chemical formulas.

A verse rule for the safe dilution of sulfuric acid is:

6. May her rest be long and placid,
    She added water to the acid.
    The other girl did what she oughter:
    She added acid to the water.

A shorter alternate:

6a. PAW!

stands for "Pour Acid into Water!"

7. (MRS.) HOF BrINCl

Initiates understand this to mean the diatomic elements Hydrogen, Oxygen, Fluorine, Bromine, Iodine, Nitrogen, and Chlorine.

8. Hearne Never Asked Kriegspiel's Extra Rent

The rare gases—Helium, Neon, Argon, Krypton, Xenon, and Radon.

9. Little Kitty Cats Nip Mother's Afghans

The activity series for replacement reactions is Lithium, Potassium (K), Calcium, Sodium (Na), Manganese, and Aluminum.

10. Henry Lit Belle Boron's Cigarette, Noting Others Fumed

The second period elements of the periodic table (also including Helium) are: Lithium, Beryllium,

Boron, Carbon, Nitrogen, Oxygen, and Fluorine. Note that for the two B words, the mnemonic uses the first two letters of Beryllium, and the whole word itself for Boron.

11. LEO GER
To Lose Electrons is Oxidation; to Gain Electrons is Reduction.

12. Soon Super Soporific Stupor Spreads
The temperature of Absolute Zero is -459.67 degrees Fahrenheit; the number of letters in each word coincides with the number to be recalled.

13. October 23 at 6:02 a.m.
The Avogadro number is 6.02×10^{23} atoms/mole.

14. Gertrude Abandoned Polonius Slain Behind The Arras.
In this mnemonic a Shakespearean theme clues the metalloids Germanium, Arsenic, Polonium, Silicon, Boron, Tellurium, and Antimony.

14a. After Taking Arsenic, Polonius Bored Gertrude Silly.
Same list, same theme, different order.

15. D.S.O.
Molecules move by Diffusion, Semipermeability, and Osmosis.

16. Frankly, Hot Lips Probably Contain Radioactive Spit.
The alkali metals are Francium, Hydrogen, Lithium, Potassium, Cesium, Rubidium, and Sodium.

17. Retching and Choking, Beryl Managed to Swallow Barium.

The alkali earth metals are Radium, Calcium, Beryllium, Magnesium, Strontium, and Barium.

Astronomy

18. Men Very Easily Make All Jobs Serve Useful Needs Promptly.

The planets, in order, starting nearest the Sun and moving out: Mercury, Venus, Earth, Mars, Asteroids, Jupiter, Saturn, Uranus, Neptune, and Pluto. In the two *M* words, the second letter of the clue word matches the second letter of the planet's name.

Variations that leave out the asteroids include:

18a. My Very Earnest Mother Just Served Us Nine Pickles.

18b. My Very Earnest Mother Just Served Us Nine Pizzas.

And, not too memorably,

18c. Men Very Easily Make Jugs Serve Useful Natural Purposes.

19. Wow! Oh Be A Fine Girl—Kiss Me Right Now, Sweetheart!

Astronomers' classification of stars in descending order of surface temperature: W, O, B, A, F, G, K, M, R, N, and S.

20. ALA DAPAMI
The "male" asteroids that cross the orbit of the earth are ALbert, ADonis, APollo, AMor, and Icarus.

21. Green Martians Love Halloween
The four "cross quarter" days when the earth is midway between the equinoxes and the solstices are Ground Hog Day (February 2), May Day (May 1), Lammas (August 1), and Halloween (October 31). A variation:

> 21a. Greek Men Love Harlots.

Biology and Zoology

Biologists who pack a knapsack and go out on a fact-finding field trip are advised to remember the following:

22. Red and yellow
> Kill a fellow.
> Red and black,
> Friend of Jack.

The color sequences that identify deadly coral snakes are red and yellow; those for the kinder (but still awful-looking) king snake are red and black.

23. Ms. Megan Maimed Six Old Reprobates Clutching Rye.
The essential differences between plants and animals are Metabolism, Mobility, Maintenance,

Structure, Organization, Reproductive Cycles, and Responsiveness.

24. GRACE'S ADMIRER

A mnemonic invented by Mike Jackson, teacher and curriculum director, Camp Lejeune, North Carolina, for the thirteen life functions, this stands for: Growth, Reproduction, Absorption, Circulation, Excretion, Secretion, Assimilation, Digestion, Movement, Ingestion, Respiration, Egestion, and Response.

25. C. HOPKINS CaFe, Mighty Good!

To decode this list of essential elements of living things, a user must know the letter symbols on the periodic table of elements: Carbon (C), Hydrogen (H), Oxygen (O), Phosphorus (P), Potassium (K), Iodine (I), Nitrogen (N), Sulfur (S), Calcium (Ca), Iron (Fe), and Magnesium (Mg). This mnemonic memorializes its inventor, one Cyril George Hopkins, who specialized in plant chemistry for over sixty years at the University of Illinois.

26. Change Master's PISSpot Cautiously.

The key elemental mineral salts required by most or all organisms (plants don't need sodium) are *Ch*lorine, *M*agnesium, *P*hosphorus, *I*ron, *S*odium, *S*ulfur, and *Ca*lcium.

27. LET

The formed elements of the blood are Leucocytes (white blood cells), Erythrocytes (red blood cells), and Thrombocytes (platelets).

28. Strange Men Slowly Crush Sinister Monsters.

The phyla in the kingdom Protista are Schizomycetes, Mastigophora, Sarcodina, Ciliophora, Sporozoa, and Myxomycetes.

29. Flu Symptoms Spread Calamity Surreptitiously.

The five classes of protozoa are Flagellata, Sarcodina, Sporozoa (all parasites), Ciliata, and Suctoria (descendents of ciliata).

30. Accident-Proof Condoms Often Are Removed Before Motherhood.

The vertebrates, arranged in eight classes, four each of two groups, are: Agnaths (lampreys), Placoderms (fish with jaws), Chondrichthyans (seawater marine species—sharks and rays), Osteichthyans (freshwater species—lungfishes, dominant aquatic animals today); and Amphibians, Reptiles, Birds, and Mammals.

31. PAL

The pancreatic and intestinal digestive enzymes are Protease, Amylase, and Lipase.

32. In the House of Creeping Florillium,
    The Yeastie Beasties are not all.
    There's molds, mushrooms, and mycelium,
    Rackety brakety fungi down the hall
    And room for toadstools by the trillium.

The different types of fungi are molds, yeasts, mushrooms and toadstools, bracket fungi, and mycelium.

33. HAT
The insect body parts are the Head, Abdomen, and Thorax.

34. Ch. C. TOADI (The Prize-Winning Frog)
The seven classes of the Phylum Arthropod are Chilopoda (centipedes), Crustacea (brine shrimp, crabs, crayfish), Trilobita (trilobites—extinct), Onychophora (peripatus), Arachnida (spiders, scorpions, ticks), Diploda (millipedes), and Insecta (bugs).

35. Great Pelican Celebration
The imaginary annual black-tie affair benefitting ugly birds represents the three most important groups of mollusks—Gastropoda, Pelecypoda, and Cephalopoda.

36. Go COrGis!
Presumably what Queen Elizabeth calls out to encourage her favorite dogs, this also represents the four kinds of great apes: Gorillas, Chimpanzees, Orangutans, and Gibbons.

37. D is for Dromedary
B is for Bactrian camel
When turned on their sides, thus ⌒⟍ and thus ⌒⌒, these two letters clue the difference between the dromedary (one hump) and the Bactrian camel (two humps).

38. Little Men in Short Black Mackintoshes:
The lesser-known arteries in the upper body of the

frog are Lingual, Mandibular, Innominate, Subclavian, Brachial, Musculocutaneous.

39. **These Ten Valuable Amino acids Have Long Preserved Life In Man.**

The ten important amino acids are Threonine, Tryptophan, Valine, Arginine, Histidine, Lysine, Phenylalanine, Leucine, Isoleucine, Methionine.

40. **Green Pond Scum Smells Dreadful—Almost Like Sauerkraut.**

The five types of algae are Green Scum on Ponds, Seaweeds, Diatoms, Algae (in) Lichens, and Stoneworts.

41. **In Persia, Men Are Tall.**

For the stages of cell division in mitosis: Interphase, Prophase, Metaphase, Anaphase, and Telophase. Without Interphase, the mnemonic becomes "Peas Make Awful Tarts."

42. **Lusty Zebras Perform Dubious Dances.**

The stages of cell division in meiosis are Leptonema, Zygonema, Pachynema, Diplonema, and Diakinesis.

43. **Old Charlie Foster Hates Women Having Dull Clothes.**

There are eight functions of the blood: Oxygen, Carbon dioxide, Food, Heat, Waste, Hormones, Disease, and Clotting.

44. See Xylem in and Phloem out.

Cambium (C = See) produces xylem cells on its inside and phloem cells on its outside.

Physical Sciences

45. ROY G. BIV

One of the best-known mnemonics of all, this cues the colors of the visible spectrum: Red, Orange, Yellow, Green, Blue, Indigo, and Violet. Variations include

45a. Richard of York Gives Battle In Vain.

45b. Real Old Yokels Guzzle Beer In Volume.

46. Department of Motor Vehicles

The formula for Density is M/V, or Density equals Mass divided by Volume.

47. MCHALES

The different forms of energy are Mechanical, Chemical, Heat, Atomic, Light, Electrical, and Solar.

48. All Hairy Men Will Buy Razors.

The constituents of soil: Air, Humus, Mineral salts, Water, Bacteria, and Rock particles.

49. Krakatoa Positively Casts Off Fumes, Generally Sulfurous Vapors.

Zoological classifications in descending order: Kingdom, Phylum, Class, Order, Family, Genus,

Species, and Variety. Variations (without *Variety!*) include:

   49a. King Philip Calls for Oodles of Fried Great Shrimp.

   49b. King Philip Comes Over For Ginger Snaps.

   49c. Kindly Professors Can Only Fail Greedy Students.

   50. Camels Often Sit Down Carefully; Perhaps Their Joints Creak. Persistent Early Oiling Might Prevent Permanent Rheumatism.

The geological time periods, in order from the oldest, are Cambrian, Ordovician, Silurian, Devonian, Carboniferous, Permian, Triassic, Jurassic, Cretaceous, Paleocene, Eocene, Oligocene, Miocene, Pliocene, Pleistocene, and Recent.

   51. Cavemen Object Strenuously During Most Polite Parties.

The time periods known as the Paleozoic Era are the Cambrian, Ordovician, Silurian, Devonian, Mississippian, Pennsylvanian, and Permian.

   52. Pass Everything Over Miss, Politely, Please, and Recently.

For the time periods known as the Cenezoic Era, which are the Paleocene, Eocene, Oligocene, Miocene, Pliocene, Pleistocene, and Recent.

   53. Ants in your pants:
       The Mites go up and
       The Tights go down.

You knew this: Stalagmites grow upward in caverns and stalagtites grow down.

54. Texas Girls Could Flirt After Others Quit To Catch Diamonds

For the Mohs' Scale of mineral hardness, from softest to hardest: Talc, Gypsum, Calcite, Fluorite, Apatite, Orthoclase, Quartz, Topaz, Corumdum, and Diamond.

At Centerville High School in Centerville, Ohio, physics teacher Howard N. Fowler has come up with a number of mnemonics that enable students to remember formulas long after they graduate. For the displacement formula

$$S = v_i t + 1/2\ at^2$$

(where S is displacement, v_i is initial velocity, t is time, a is acceleration, and the second t is time elapsed), he has students visualize the following:

55. S = 0 ⊓ (a vitamin plus half a T-square)

For Newton's universal law of gravitation, or

$$F = \frac{Gm_o\ \ \ m_e}{R^2}$$

which refers to the specific force the Earth has on a mass near its surface (F stands for gravitational force between two objects, G is the universal gravitational constant; m_o is mass of the object; m_e is the Earth mass; and the R is the separation between two masses), his students read

56. F = Gee, Mommy, Over separation between centers squared.

The jingle rhyme

57. Six point six seven
    Times ten to minus eleven.
    Newton meter squared
    Per kilogram squared.

helps them remember the value and units of G and works best when set to a familiar tune.

Botany

58. Leaflets three? Let it be!
This is a rule of thumb for identifying poison ivy plants.

59. MADCAP Horse
Trees and shrubs with opposite branching are Maple, Ash, Dogwood, Caprifoliacea (the family that includes the honeysuckle and viburnum), and Horse (Chestnut).

60. Sedges have edges,
    Rushes are round.
    Grasses have nodes,
    And much abound!

In plant identification this tells how to distinguish between sedges and rushes.

61. Cyril Saw Fern Gouge Connor's Corvette.
Gymnosperms (seed plants, not flowers) comprise Cycadeoids (and Cycads), Seed Ferns, Ginkgos, Conifers, and Cordaites.

Naval Science

62. Red right returning.
This is an alliterative sailor's mnemonic for returning to port, when the red markers should be on the starboard side (the right side) of the boat.

63. Port is left;
   Starboard is right.
For landlubbers who can't remember which is port and which is starboard, but who can connect the fact that the word *port*, like the word *left*, has four letters.

64. Even Red Nuns have Odd Black Cans.
Sailors know that red nun buoys are even-numbered; black can buoys are odd-numbered.

65. Timid Virgins Make Dull Company.
In navigation true north is by the stars (which can't be seen in daylight); magnetic north differs according to magnetic variation (the lines of force on the globe, which change from one area to another); and the boat's compass reading for north

fluctuates according to its own variables (say, a big hunk of iron sitting near it). To locate where a boat is on a chart, a sailor calculates True (North), Variation, Magnetic (force), Deviation, and Compass (reading).

NINE

Accessing
the Computer Memory

It was my intention, on beginning this book, to ferret out what I assumed would be hordes of computer mnemonics—clever little jingles and acronyms that people use to get into their programs. I know it took me weeks to learn the admittedly simple keyboard formula that gets me in and out of my own word processor.

But it seems no one else has such elementary problems. Bernard Tanner, an old friend and former English teacher turned technical writer for a computer company, told me that you don't need mnemonics when you have computers because computers remember everything for you.

I still think it helps to remember how to get the computer to tell what it knows; my own mnemonic for getting into my WordPerfect program is

1. ABBA White Plains

which stands for "A prompt: B, B prompt A:WP."
(White Plains is the city where I have my office.)

But except for this desperate attempt to master
the comparatively simple ins and outs of my program, I turned up only one computer mnemonic,
courtesy of the ever-cheerful Mike Jackson in
Camp Lejeune, North Carolina:

2. CAD

For rebooting in many IBM-compatible programs,
press down the Control, Alternate, and Delete
keys simultaneously.

TEN

Mnemonics for Daily Living, or, Even Professors Have to Set Their Clocks for Daylight Saving Time

This is my favorite section, because the mnemonics here are for the kind of facts that every one of us needs to know. They remind us that we all—historians, poets, good and bad spellers, lawyers, musicians, mathematicians, doctors, scientists, and computer-inputters—live in the same world, breathe the same air, and struggle with the same realities.

So here, with feeling and friendship, and with a sense of appreciation and gratitude to all the lovely people who were so cheerful and happy to help me with this collection, are ways to stay on top of the demands of daily living.

1. Spring forward, fall back.

This famous mnemonic is an easy way to remember how to set clocks when daylight saving time begins and ends.

2. When it's Sunday in San Francisco, it's Monday in Manila.

A nifty way to remember which date it is on either side of the International Date Line.

3. No need for confusion if we but recall
    That Easter on the first Sunday after the
    Full moon following the vernal equinox
    Doth fall.

Honest—this mnemonic *is* memorable if you say it over a few times, and it not only explains when the day of Easter will fall but puts us in touch with the earth's cycles.

4. Hideous Fools and Morons, Keep Silent!

This is a checklist for ensuring that children look presentable; it includes Hair, Face, Midsection, Knees, and finally Shoes.

5. Beatrice Rides Yonder, Over the Great Plains.

The primary and secondary colors, respectively, are Blue, Red, and Yellow, and Orange, Green, and Purple.

6. Better Be Prepared, Scout.

This is a Boy Scout mnemonic for the order of priority in giving first aid: Breathing, Bleeding, Poisoning, and Shock.

7. Smart Women Deplore Keeping Accounts.

The things to check when leaving the house are the Stove, the Windows, the Door, the Keys, and the Alarm. An alternate version, reversing Keys and Door, is

7a. Smart Women Keep Denying Adultery.

8. Great Alexander's Army Devastated Enemy Persians (who) Relinquished Prizes Seized On The Tiber.

The birthstones, in chronological order from January to December, are Garnet, Amethyst, Aquamarine, Diamond, Emerald, Pearl, Ruby, Peridot, Sapphire, Opal, Topaz, and Turquoise.

9. FiFi

This little dog helps absentminded cooks remember, when coating chicken fillets in flour and egg, which coating comes first: First the Flour (then the egg).

10. Righty, tighty; lefty, loosy.

Turn bolts to the right to make them tighter, to the left to loosen them.

ACKNOWLEDGMENTS

This book is like Ringo Starr of the Beatles—it got by with a little help from friends—and Blanche in Tennessee Williams's *A Streetcar Named Desire*—it depended on the kindness of strangers. I am much indebted to friends, including expert mnemonics users in my family and Stephen Booth, whose great kindness always springs forward and never falls back.

Beth Harrison, M.D., and Rickie Harrison, M.D., provided the funniest medical mnemonics. I am grateful for the kindness of Mike Jackson, J. Gardiner Pieper, and Robert Bloomfield, M.D., who took time out of their busy schedules to help me in the areas of science, law, and medicine. Margot Slade of *The New York Times* first interested me in mnemonics outside my own field. I would like to thank Sheila Curry, whose idea this book was, and Kevin Smith, who saw that it became one.

The complete list of everyone who contributed is long.

Barbara A. Achenbaum, math teacher and department chair, the Masters School, Dobbs Ferry, New York; author of *Geometry in Rhyme* (unpublished).

Andrew Appel, harpsichordist, New York, New York.

Jules Bernard, attorney, Washington, D.C.

Richard Besley, M.D., White Plains, New York.

Robert Bloomfield (see Sources)

Stephen Booth, professor, Department of English, University of California at Berkeley.

Victoria Brademan, attorney, New York, New York.

Carmen Cole and Dick Holt and their children— Derek, Richard, Jenny, and James; Ontario, Canada.

Dr. Crypton (see Sources) and his go-between, Jessica Snyder, of *Science Digest.*

Harry L. Dangel, D.Ed., Department of Special Education, Georgia State University, Atlanta, Georgia.

Louise Edmonds, the Masters School, Dobbs Ferry, New York.

Matthew Ferraro, son.

Mimi Ferraro, daughter.

Howard N. Fowler, physics teacher, Centerville High School, Centerville, Ohio.

Charlie Garfinckle, salesman emeritus, Mount Vernon, New York.

Dr. Stephen Gerstman, D.D.S., Tarrytown, New York.

Dr. Allan Gold, school psychologist, San Francisco, California.

The Goldfried family—Dr. Billy, Linda, Adam, Jenny, and Evan—White Plains, New York.

Richard Halperin, attorney, New York, New York.

Beth Harrison, M.D., and Rickie Harrison, M.D., Chappaqua, New York.

Don Harrison, Harrison Enterprises, San Diego, California.

Mike Jackson, Curriculum Direction, Dependents' School, Camp Lejeune, North Carolina.

Mike Jackson's classroom students.

E. A. Kline, Washington, D.C.

J. W. McAuliffe, masterful Latin teacher, the Hackley School, Tarrytown, New York.

Elaine and Sohier Marks, mariners, Rye, New York.

Dr. Richard Monte, professor of classics, University of Wisconsin.

Paul Morris, advertising, Tempe, Arizona.

J. Gardiner Pieper, *Pieper Law Review,* New York, New York.

Mary Ray, nurse, New York, New York.

Dr. Judah Roher, M.D., White Plains, New York.

Rebecca Ross, photography teacher, Tempe, Arizona.

Emily Silverman, the Masters School, Dobbs Ferry, New York.

Margot Slade, editor, "Education Life," *The New York Times.*

Susan Kelz Sperling, writer and teacher, Rye, New York.

Murray Suid, writer, teacher, mnemonist, Palo Alto, California; author of *Demonic Mnemonics: 800 Spelling Tricks for 800 Tricky Words* (Belmont, Calif.: David S. Lake Publishers, 1981).

Bernard Tanner, F. Scott Fitzgerald expert and computer maven, Palo Alto, California.

Deryn Thomas, the Hackley School, Tarrytown, New York.

SOURCES

Books

Bloomfield, Robert L., M.D.; and E. Ted Chandler, M.D. *Mnemonics Rhetoric and Poetics for Medics.* Winston-Salem, N.C.: Harbinger Press, 1982.

Bloomfield, Robert L., M.D.; and Carolyn F. Pedley, M.D. *More Mnemonics Rhetoric and Poetics for Medics.* Volume 2. Winston-Salem, N.C.: Harbinger Press, 1984.

Brett, Simon, Editor. *The Faber Book of Useful Verse.* London: Faber & Faber, 1981.

A Dictionary of Mnemonics. London: Eyre Methuen Ltd., 1972.

Halacy, Don. *How to Improve Your Memory.* New York: Franklin Watts, 1977.

Articles

Crypton, Dr. (pseudonym). "Timid Virgins Make Dull Company." *Science Digest,* June 1983.

Dangel, Harry L. "Promoting Writing STARS." *Academic Therapy* 23, no. 3 (January 1988).

Jackson, Michael C.; and Norman D. Anderson. "ROY G. BIV Never Forgets." *The Science Teacher,* February 1988.

Jones, Landon Y., Jr. "Never Lower Tillie's Pants, Mother Might Come Home." *Esquire,* September 1974.

Levin, Joel R. "A Concrete Strategy for Remembering Abstract Prose." *American Education Research Journal,* Summer 1983.

Stone, Judith. "Homer's Greatest Hits." *Discover,* September 1989.

INDEX OF MNEMONICS

Chapter 1: History

Broken Cesspools Emit Smells (28)
CABAL (18)
Can Queen Victoria Eat Cold Apple Pie? (31)
Carol Died Clutching (19)
Catch Queen Victoria Eating Cold Apple Pie
   (31)
Cats Catch Vile Bugs (19)
Columbus sailed the ocean blue (19)
Crazed Chipmunks Jump Past Nubile Koalas
   (28)
Divorced, beheaded, died (16)
Do Men Ever Visit Boston? (19)
Excellent Gents Remain Bodaciously Cool (29)
Four *F*'s, The (25)
Gentle Virgins Who Marry (22)
George the Third said with a smile (16)
HOMES (26)
In sixteen hundred sixty-six (16)
In the 730s, at the Battle of Tours (19)
Is Perpetual Zeal The Means? (23)
Kiss That Sheila Allowed, The (25)
Naked Amazons Mumbling Mayhem Rally
   Round (29)
NASA's Astronaut Enjoys Aussie Affairs Again
   (28)
Newly Structured Quadrangles (30)
No Plan Like Yours To Study History Wisely
   (18)
Not Yearning For Mary's Virginal Devotion (27)
Poor Queen Victoria Eats Crow At Christmas
   (31)
POSH (26)
Practice Gives Boys Confidence (24)
Randy Orangutans Take Care During Sex (25)

Chapter 2: Language

Chapter 3: Spelling

*E*ating *Ch*ocolates is *S*ublime! (51)
*E*ditors alt*e*r *e*ditions (50)
*E*lectricity strikes out (52)
Embarrassment of *ri*che*s* in *r*'s and *s*'s, An (51)
*E*nvelop*e* is *s*ealed on both *e*nds, An (51)
*G*eorge's *E*lderly *O*ld *G*randfather (49)
*Geo*rge *G*reedily *R*avishes Annabelle (49)
Hyg*i*enic *G.I.* Joe (52)
I before *e* (48)
I *e*at a cass*e*role (49)
I have a preference for ease (52)
*I'm mi*grating south for the winter (52)
It's not a finished *bridge* (49)
I write Re: *commend*ations (53)
John Rockefeller's *son Nel*son (52)
Jud*gm*ents for and against *G*eneral *M*otors (52)
Knowle*dge d*epends on *d*ata (52)
Lend me a cal*end*ar (51)
*L*ittle *F*este in *Twelfth Night* (53)
Lop off the *e* (51)
Neither leisured foreign counterfeiter (48)
P*olo* is for the frivo*lo*us rich (52)
Pre*tense* makes me *tense* (53)
Princip*al* is your pal, The (49)
Privi*leg*e gives a *leg* up in life (53)
*P*ublic *r*elations *offers* (53)
Put the *Chi*cken in the *Ca*r (48)
*R*at *I*n *T*he *H*ouse *M*ay *E*at *T*he *I*ce *C*ream, *A* (48)
Ray of sun will drive away the *gray*, A (52)
Silver (*Ag*) Weight (*gra*vity) (50)
Station*e*ry uses *e*nvelopes (49)
*T*all *H*ero *L*oves *E*legant *T*ight *E*lastics, *A* (50)
Too many qui*zz*es make me di*zz*y (53)

Chapter 4: Math

Chapter 5: Music

Chapter 6: Law

Chapter 7: Anatomy and Medicine

Chapter 8: Sciences

Chapter 9: Computers

Chapter 10: Everyday Living